SURVIVING THE DARKNESS

SURVIVING THE DARKNESS

GRACE M.D. KETTERMAN

THOMAS NELSON PUBLISHERS
Nashville

Published in Nashville, Tennessee, by Oliver-Nelson Books, a division of Thomas Nelson, Inc., Publishers, and distributed in Canada by Word Communications, Richmond, British Columbia.

Unless otherwise noted, the Bible version used in this publication is THE NEW KING JAMES VERSION. Copyright © 1979, 1980, 1982, Thomas Nelson, Inc., Publishers.

Scripture quotation noted PHILLIPS is from J. B. Phillips: THE NEW TESTAMENT IN MODERN ENGLISH, Revised Edition. © J. B. Phillips 1958, 1960, 1972. Used by permission of Macmillan Publishing Co., Inc.

Library of Congress Cataloging-in-Publication Data

Ketterman, Grace H.
    [Depression hits every family]
    Surviving the Darkness / Grace Ketterman.
        p.   cm.
    Originally published: Depression hits every family. Nashville : Oliver Nelson, © 1988.
    Includes bibliographical references.
    ISBN 0-8407-9275-1 (pbk.)
    1. Depression, Mental   I. Title.
[RC537.K47   1993]
616.85'27—dc20   93–5899
                                                                 CIP

Printed in the United States of America.

1 2 3 4 5 6 — 98 97 96 95 94 93

CONTENTS

PREFACE

Her face and entire body displayed her shock and fear as Joyce came to her mother one autumn evening for help. Seeing her sensitive thirteen-year-old's face was enough to stop dinner preparations. Mother left the kitchen and sat soberly with her daughter who had just finished reading Orwell's book, *1984.*[1]

"Tell me, Mother," Joyce pleaded, "that such things will never happen! I don't want to live in a world like that!" The book, all too prophetically, describes a world in which people become emotionally hardened and incapable of compassion. A world, it reveals, that is mechanized and orderly but cold and indescribably lonely.

Joyce's mother, with the deepest sincerity, reassured her. Humankind was made in God's image, and God *is* love. Therefore, rest assured, she affirmed, such a world can hardly happen. And she believed her own words, reassured her child's fears, and resumed the preparation of dinner.

Not long after that eventful evening, however, Joyce's mother learned of a startling study done by Dr. Colin M. Turnbull.[2] The British anthropologist had discovered a tribe of people, known as the Ik people, in Africa. They had been removed from their natural, ages-old habitat in the mountains. That area had become a national

1. Eric Blair [George Orwell], *1984* (New York: Harcourt, 1949).
2. Colin M. Turnbull, *The Mountain People* (New York: Simon and Schuster, 1972).

park or game preserve, and the Ik people were forcibly transplanted to the plains. They grieved the loss of the familiar places for a time, but settled into their new homes. None of their tribal rituals or religious practices seemed to "fit" the arid flatness of their new home.

In the incredibly brief span of only fourteen years, the happy, loving people became a debased tribe. They stopped teasing and pampering their aged grandparents. They made no efforts to comfort the sick or suffering. Anyone unable to keep pace with the others was left alone to die. Dr. Turnbull's studies were full of examples of total selfishness and loss of caring.

"Could it be," Joyce's mother asked herself, "that this is the point of Orwell's book?" She decided, "But that is what one would expect from a 'heathen' country."

Then she thought about the screaming headlines of individuals attacked, robbed, abused, or killed by another human being in the United States. And such events, increasingly, were being perpetrated within the sight and hearing of onlookers, but no one risked a rescue.

Such tragic crimes occur with accelerating frequency. It is, indeed, the scenario of *1984*—and more. And all of us must face the decade that is depicted as it is being lived—an era of depression, rage, and multiplying crime and suicide, the expressions of that rage.

Accompanying suicides is a long list of other debilitating symptoms and signs of serious trouble in the world of the 1990s. Alcoholism and drug addiction continue to increase despite heroic educational efforts.

Suicides in children from five to fourteen years old increased from 0.3 per 100,000 children to 0.6, not a shocking number, but double in twelve years. In young people from fifteen to twenty-four years old, the rate increased from 8.8 deaths to 16 per 100,000—again almost doubling in that same twelve-year period (1970 to 1982).[3]

Suicides follow accidents and homicides as the leading causes

3. U.S. National Center for Health Statistics, *Vital Statistics of the United States,* Annual, 1986, Table No. 122.

of death in teenagers. Many researchers believe there are "hidden" suicides in both of the other causes of death. If these could be verified, it is almost certain that suicide would be *the* leading cause of teenage deaths.[4]

School failures and dropouts continue to concern schoolteachers and administrators. Students' academic achievement scores drop consistently despite attempts of devoted staff members to prepare their students to do well.

Depression is many-faceted in its demonstration. It may be blatant or covered, clear or disguised, *temporary or chronic*. It is a frighteningly increasing illness of our time.

Until the 1960s, most child psychiatrists denied the existence of depression in preadolescent children, often because they simply did not recognize its unique expression. But a study in 1983 of nine-year-olds showed that 1.8 percent were suffering a *major* depression disorder, and 3 to 4 percent had the symptoms of *minor* depression.[5]

In adults, too, depression is a leading ailment, contributing to loss of time on the job and helping fill our mental hospitals. It results in distress and disharmony in the family as well as within the individual.

Those who seek answers to this widespread problem look in several directions. Those who have discovered the quick cure of newly researched medications believe that much, if not most, depression is endogenous. That is, it is due to a biochemical imbalance in the body, resulting from hormones secreted by the body's complex endocrine system. And indeed such chemical changes can be demonstrated in laboratory animals as well as in human beings.

Another type of depression, to them, is exogenous, which is a person's reaction to events. This is sometimes called *reactive depression* and occurs, for example, as a response to a loss such as a death. Those who study human behaviors believe that depression is learned and is a result of conditioned responses.

4. James P. Comer, M.D., "Young Suicides," *Parents,* August 1982, p. 88.
5. J. H. Kashani et al., "Depression in Children," *Archives of General Psychology,* vol. 40, November 1983, p. 1222.

The adherents of psychoanalysis attribute depression to inner conflicts that stem from childhood experiences. These events, they believe, are forgotten or "repressed" into the unconscious part of the mind and only the emotions are felt as depression.

Developmental psychology teaches that early childhood losses, during certain stages of personality development, create a likelihood of depression later on. Whatever the theory, each school of thought has done extensive research and is equally convinced of its own method of treatment.

The unending debate of these varied and sincere groups of researchers is not the focal point of this book, however. Instead I intend to clarify the common manifestations of depression. By recognizing these at an early stage, most people can define the factors or events that precipitated their depression, and they can, therefore, obtain help and "recover" more rapidly; they can be better prepared to help others in this regard, too.

In different age groups, depression may express itself in varying patterns. Therefore, we will consider its most common manifestations and causes—physical, emotional, social, and psychological—characteristic of each age group. And we will look at some useful information regarding its treatment.

INTRODUCTION: WHAT CAUSES DEPRESSION?

Since there are several schools of thought regarding the cause of depression and, consequently, its treatment, let's examine some of them as well as my own theory about the subject. The current thinking ranges from the classic psychoanalytic to a simplistic "pooh-pooh" attitude.

Psychoanalytic Theory

Psychoanalytic theory asserts that depression is rooted in childhood experiences that have been "repressed" or locked away in the subconscious part of an individual's personality. The old experiences, endured painfully during a period in life when a person is relatively helpless, leave a pervasive sense of sadness, helplessness, guilt, fear, and anger. When new events occur that are similar to the old childhood experiences, the same old feelings emerge. Because people often fail to recognize the similarity between current events and old ones, they cannot connect the depression with its current cause and only feel very sad and hopeless. Current research does seem convincing about early life experiences regarding parent-child relations and their impact on depression.[1]

1. D. J. Burbach and C. M. Borduin, "Parent-Child Relations and the Etiology of Depression," *Clinical Psychology Review,* vol. 6, 1986, pp. 133–153.

Genetic Theory

According to another theory, a person may inherit depression just as he inherits blue eyes or brown hair. We know that children of depressed parents are more likely to suffer from depression, attention deficit disorders (ADD), separation anxiety, and other emotional or behavioral problems than those whose parents are not seriously depressed. But this theory seems abhorrent to me because the depressed person is left relatively hopeless about recovery.

Those who accept this genetic theory spend a great deal of effort seeking medications that can relieve some of the emotional pain of the depression. But they may overlook the habits learned from an environment that was at times full of anger, fear, or the pain of loss of some kind. (Recent studies of adopted children offer evidence that events taking place in a child's life have a greater influence on the possibility of depression than does the genetic factor.)[2] Therefore, sufferers may become dependent on the pills that numb the pain but fail to gain insight and knowledge to guide them to the road to true recovery.

Cognitive Theory

The cognitive theory maintains that depression is the result of faulty information. Due to problems relating to the development of the ability to think and understand, children learn early in life to be depressed. They may learn this attitude and behavior from parents or others who are depressed and may copy their responses to life. Or they may learn from an occasional experience of sadness that this emotion is sure to gain for them a great deal of comfort and attention.

These people grow up looking for disasters in life and responding to them with tears and mourning. Almost always, they find a kind and nurturing person who will feel sorry for them and try to help them feel better.

2. Paul V. Trad, *Infant and Childhood Depression* (New York: John Wiley & Sons, 1987), p. 214.

Sue was such a girl. She was a naturally sensitive, sunny child who was easy to love and transparent with all her feelings. Her mother, a very nurturing woman, unwittingly found pleasure in sharing Sue's many emotions, and she especially enjoyed comforting her daughter. Whether it was a Band-Aid for a scraped knee or sympathy for a wounded spirit, Sue was quickly better and warmly appreciative.

In the dramatic years of adolescence, Sue's pain over broken friendships, difficult teachers, or knotty school subjects became burdensome. Her mother realized that she had helped create a teenager who was becoming a candidate for a depressive personality. She gradually stopped feeling sorry for Sue and helped her think more about solutions and less about emotions.

One day, Sue returned from school after a truly miserable day. She discarded her books, threw herself dramatically on the sofa, and wailed. Despite her new resolve, Mother left her sewing and knelt beside her suffering daughter. But none of her comforting techniques seemed to work, and Sue cried on. Mother, finally, sat silently beside her.

To her mother's amazement, Sue stopped her tears, became thoughtful, and said with some surprise, "You know, Mom, I think I kind of like feeling bad!" What a healing discovery! Sue could now find a simple cure for her *learned* habit of depression, and that was to *think* of solutions and to ask for loving attention whenever she needed it rather than seek it through depressed feelings.

Physical or Biochemical Causes

Several physical factors can contribute to genuine depression or may so closely resemble it that sufferers believe themselves to be depressed. It is extremely important that you know enough about these complex entities to realize the value of a careful physical evaluation if you are even minimally depressed.

By all odds, the most common example of physically induced depression is the condition now commonly known as PMS—the premenstrual syndrome so annoying to women. For a few days to as long as ten days or more each month, the changes in the body's hormone cycles carry a powerful psychological charge. A woman may gradually or suddenly feel irritable, become short-tempered and moody, and experience changes in eating and sleeping habits. Perhaps most difficult to bear is the sense of absolute hopelessness—the world is an unbearable place; it cannot get better.

Miraculously, shortly after the onset of the menstrual cycle, the PMS sufferer awakens to a sense of peace that slowly grows to a feeling of well-being and even exuberance in wonderful contrast to the gloomy despair of the previous day or two. She is delightedly "cured," that is, until next month.

Decreased functioning of the thyroid gland may make people believe they are depressed. They are chronically fatigued, have difficulty concentrating, and do not function efficiently on the job or in social situations. They tend to sleep a lot and usually gain weight.

Too much thyroxin, one of the hormones secreted by the thyroid gland, on the other hand, may give persons excessive energy. Their pulse rate increases, the muscles may become tense, and they often lose weight. To others, they seem nervous and anxious.

Less than two decades ago, medical science had identified some twenty hormones. It is estimated now that there may be ten times that many.[3] Scientists recognize the impact of hormones on all bodily functions, and they are closer to comprehending the interaction of the mind and emotions with these intricate chemicals.

Depressed people have increased amounts of certain hormones. Schizophrenic people have a different balance in their hormonal levels from that of nonschizophrenics. And an acquaintance of mine is currently studying the hormone levels of college-age young people who have just broken off a relationship with a sweetheart. He expects to be able to predict, for example, if they are depressed (grieving) enough to make them suicidal.

Those who are most knowledgeable about the body's complex endocrine (hormone-secreting glands) system are most likely to discuss stress as a major factor in depression. That stress triggers biochemical responses is beyond debate. In fact I picture these glands with their vast numbers of secretions as being like a carefully

3. "A User's Guide to Hormones," *Newsweek,* 12 January 1987, p. 50.

aligned string of dominoes. Stress is the finger that needs to touch only a single block, which knocks down the entire chain.

It is logical that these hormones may accumulate to high levels, they may be neutralized by other chemicals, or they may be metabolized to lower levels than normal. When, for whatever reason, imbalances occur, there will be physical or emotional symptoms or both.

The argument about whether depression is caused by a chemical imbalance or is due to stress becomes resolved. Stress triggers the chemical chain reaction. And that, in turn, affects a person's mood or attitude.

When you add to this information the learned habit patterns of your childhood, you can very well understand what determines stress for you. Life situations and personal dilemmas that concerned my grandmother and my parents became my own. And these concerns produce anxiety or fear, which creates stress, which triggers the body's chemical responses. And so the cycle closes and reacts upon itself.

Let me review and coordinate these concepts for you in my own fashion.

My Own Theory

For many years in my varying medical experiences I have worked with depressed people. I have observed closely, read and listened a great deal, and tried to put together the many theories about depression.

In addition, over twenty years ago, I realized that I was becoming depressed. After trying in vain to cure my problems, I did what any logical person should do. I went to a doctor who specialized in emotional problems. In a relatively short time, I learned basic concepts that transformed my emotional life. Without a doubt, subjective experience, enlightened by the objective wisdom of that exceptional doctor, taught me more than books or research, important as they are.

I believe that a group of influences intermingle to create the painful and complex entity of depression. Let's investigate them.

1. *Genetic predispostion*. Research is still unable to prove this beyond a doubt as it has in the diagnoses of schizophrenia and manic-depressive (called bipolar) illnesses. But we may safely assume that the endocrine system and neurological equipment are hereditary. We know that people are born with lesser or greater energy, higher or lower intelligence (though other influences may alter that), and a more or less sensitive nervous system.

   So we can see that an intelligent, highly sensitive person who pours out adrenaline under stress will respond one way to life situations. This individual is likely to think out answers, fight for solutions, and end up with a sense of confidence that will win over depression.

   On the other hand, a person who inherits a good brain but thinks more slowly, has a low-functioning endocrine system, and is not especially sensitive to stress may react to it with calmness or indifference.

   Hardly anyone falls into either extreme, however. Most of us lie somewhere in between, so we may be very sensitive and bright but have a low energy level. We simply cannot cope, physically, with stressful situations. We are more likely to feel the frustration and helplessness that are elements of depression.

   When certain elements are present in the body in high concentration, we tend to feel a certain way. If other substances are present in the brain or around the nerve endings, we are likely to feel differently. Scientists have been able to manufacture medications that will make most people feel very much as they want to feel. I hope you will agree with me that biologically inherited factors certainly are important in creating or preventing depression.

2. *Family practices and beliefs*. Among relatives and friends in the close-knit small community where I grew up, I observed many important forces at work. In retrospect, I see how vital these factors were in molding my attitudes, feelings, and activities. They essentially determined my beliefs about people, my world, and myself. The influences from my family taught love, compassion, tenderness, and the value of education, work, and

achievement. However, there also were some areas of excessive rigidity, worry, and depression in the adults of my "clan." I daresay that no family has found a perfect balance. All my siblings, nevertheless, became productive, compassionate people who tried to make our small areas of the world good ones.

A schoolmate of mine came from a family with different values. She was intelligent, but her family did not value education. She seemed socially at ease, but her family was a private one—almost reclusive. I never knew anyone in her family to reach out to someone in need. In fact, I suspect they were afraid of people. This person of high potential quit high school after becoming pregnant, married prematurely, and has led a life of little impact on her personal world. This young woman was probably so constricted by the limits of her family that she was angry, sad, and helpless. I suspect she felt guilty over her unplanned pregnancy, and I can almost certainly predict she has been depressed.

I suggest you review your family background. Try to recall the general emotional state of your parents, grandparents, and close relatives. Recapture, if you can, their beliefs about the important issues of your life—religion, politics, you, and themselves. How did they feel toward their neighbors or one another? Did these examples or teachings encourage you to feel optimistic, safe, loving, and kind? Or do you recall more fear, frustration, and futility regarding you and your future? Did you learn to be depressed or cheerful?

After you take this backward look, return to your present. What are you teaching your children? How do you feel most of the time? How would you *like* to feel? You can choose!

3. *Impact of the environment.* Family influences, I believe, create the core of beliefs, emotions, and self-concept that predispose individuals to depression or health. Nevertheless, many other people and events can modify this.

I was the only person in my grade for the eight years I attended a rural grade school. I had little competition and few ways of knowing whether I was stupid or bright, although I suspected the latter. What a shock it was to enter the ninth grade in a school with some two hundred students in my freshman class! I did not dress, act, or feel like any of them, and I still recall the terror of those early weeks.

I made myself as unobtrusive as possible, though I did study hard. When we received our grade cards after the first six weeks, to my horror I read a *C* in social studies. I had never before received such a low grade, so I summoned all my courage and confronted Miss Smith. Why had I gotten a low grade, and how could I improve?

I have never forgotten the contempt with which she looked at me, a frightened country girl. She hastily assured me there was nothing wrong with a *C* and turned away to end the discussion. I knew she believed that I was capable of only average work, and she had no time for me. Fortunately I proved her wrong, though she never said anything to me when I improved my grade.

Working as I have with public schools, I have seen many "Miss Smiths." Out of their attitudes of indifference or cynicism, they expect too little; knowingly or not, they hold their students in some disdain; and all too often they get what they expect! Next to parents, teachers have the greatest influence on children's lives.

Fortunately, the Miss Smiths are far outnumbered by teachers who truly care about their students, who not only teach academic topics but help parents teach respect and consideration. These devoted people deserve great credit for going far beyond the call of duty.

The treatment children receive from neighbors, Sunday school teachers, youth leaders, and other adults adds to their self-concepts. A positive influence will encourage health, but a negative one will promote some degree of depression.

A deprived environment is likely to create limitations. Most people who grow up in impoverished areas seem to merge into those patterns of poverty and dependency with poor self-esteem and personal depression. Occasionally, however, an individual manages to escape the manacles of such a community.

Some researchers studied such unexpectedly successful people from a large city. They asked these persons what had enabled them to escape their surroundings and "make it." Almost everyone quickly identified a single person whose example had become the turning point of their lives.[4]

One example was a woman who had managed to become an elementary schoolteacher. She came from a family poisoned by alcoholism and violence, which was fairly typical of the families in her neighborhood. At home she received little tenderness and no encouragement to learn or hope to improve her lot.

In her third grade in school, she had one of those beautiful teachers who conveyed love and a desire to help her students want to learn. As a reward for good study habits for a week, the teacher had a special story time every Friday when she would read about heroes and heroines who overcame difficulties to find successes.

Over the period of that year, this woman had made with increasing determination the decision to become just like her wonderful teacher. And she did.

One person, over a period of nine months, was instrumental in helping one child overcome the depression of her environment and her very life. How much easier and more economical it is to prevent depression, or relieve it early, than to treat it later on.

4. *The stress factor*. Stress, according to the science of physics, is a force acting upon a resisting object with the resulting creation of strain within that object. A strong wind, for example, blowing against a tree will cause it to bend. The wind is the stress; the bending of the tree evidences the strain. If a tree is old, weak, or brittle, it is likely to break under the force of strong wind. Or if the wind is strong enough, as in a hurricane or a tornado, even the toughest and healthiest of trees may break.

4. Robert Couchman, M.Ed., Executive Director of Metro Toronto Family Service Association, "Against All Odds: An Examination of the Significant Other Person Factor in the Education of Disadvantaged Children" (Paper prepared for the professional development day of Hamilton inner city school elementary teachers, December 1975).

And so it is with people. Those who have inherited a certain set of physical conditions, who have learned a particular system of beliefs from their families, and who have experienced a special combination of events from their total environment will respond to stress according to those factors. This response will be better or worse depending on the balance and combination among the influences.

Furthermore, the particular events of life that become stressful are in some degree taught by parents. My father found it essential to be on time. I worry if I may be late. My mother fussed a good deal over entertaining guests. I found it difficult to have company in my home until I learned how to overcome this. Stress will be further determined by each individual's boss, spouse, children, and friends.

Although this is not a book on stress, you should understand something about it and its influence on your body, feelings, and thoughts. It is easier for me to comprehend stress if I think of earlier times and a simpler, if not safer, life-style.

My grandmother once told me a story of living on the plains of Kansas when Indians roamed at will. They were usually (and understandably) angry with the encroaching white people who steadily claimed their lands, killed their wildlife, and rejected their life-style. So it was common for the Indians to steal and kill in return.

One day a small group of these Indians came to her isolated farm home, demanded entry, and proceeded to help themselves to her food supplies. She described the panic that hit her. Her heart pounded, and she felt like screaming and running away. Despite her pacifist beliefs, she wished she had a gun with which to protect her family. Her faith and courage enabled her to help them gather the food she had, and finally they stalked away as silently as they had arrived.

Stress is the Creator's provision for the preservation of life. When a wild animal or invading human threatened people like my grandparents, their instincts told them to fight or flee. Today we call this reaction to stress the *fight or flight phenomenon,* and it still universally occurs.

The problem in today's complex world is this: stress is rare caused by the attack of a wild animal or an Indian. It is caused by fear of disapproval and rejection. A friend quarrels, and we fear the loss of that relationship. A spouse ignores us, leaving us feeling inferior and unworthy. The boss is displeased with our work. Could he fire (reject) us? Our children rebel against our rules. What if they, like others, run away?

How can we fight or escape stresses? Our newspaper headlines almost daily reveal the attempts of people to fight their supposed enemies through violence and even murder. People still run away from home, jobs, or responsibilities. But even these instinctive responses do not solve the problem or relieve the stress.

And those who patiently or helplessly attempt to stand still, like my grandmother did with her uninvited guests, and endure the stress are hardly better off. They often end up with severe physical illnesses due basically to stress, or they become depressed.

Stress stimulates the adrenal glands, which produce hormones that act upon the entire body. The hormones cause the heart to pump faster and harder to supply plenty of blood to the muscles. They provide amazing strength to those muscles for use in fighting or fleeing if necessary; they send messages to the lungs and cause them to work harder to bring fresh oxygen to the blood and remove the waste product carbon dioxide. And they create responses from other glands to back them up, so to speak.

Everything physically is set to function efficiently. But when we can't run or fight, what becomes of all these bodily functions? In a sense they are frozen, and the hormones simply circulate. They may, then, cause much of the biochemical imbalance that results in depression. But equally significant are the helplessness and the frustration we experience through this often infuriating type of stress.

It may be tempting to use medications to counteract this biochemical melee. They can help us *feel* better. And there is a place for medications, but we'll discuss that later on.

One of the answers to the stress-and-strain phenomenon is that of planned, vigorous exercise. Even if such physical activity must be postponed and cannot be acted upon at the moment the stress occurs, it will somewhat relieve the tension, will create better bodily functioning, and may well improve the depression. Many people will testify to feeling emotionally very good after a brisk walk or swim. This makes excellent sense physiologically because the exercise metabolizes the adrenaline and gets rid of it for the time being.

The causes of depression, then, really need not be debated. Certainly there are inherited, genetic factors. Absolutely there are learned habits of behaving, reacting, and feeling that are taught within families. All of us are influenced by environment, how cold or warm is the climate, and how kind or fearsome are the people. And all of us know something about stress.

I could diagram these four powerful forces like this:

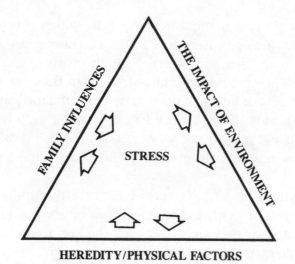

Each is connected with and interacts intricately with all the others.

You must understand each of these forces within your life. Then you can begin to gain control of them and find the resources for putting your life in a healthy balance. You need not stay depressed!

The Many Faces of Depression

Depression in all ages is a creeping sickness that we continue to learn about. Early in my psychiatric training, a mentor whom I respect immensely taught me that depression is a complex mixture, not a simple entity. It is made up of varying proportions of fear, anger, sadness, helplessness, guilt, remorse and, sometimes, hopelessness.

Although most people are aware of the feelings of sadness and helplessness associated with depression, the anger, guilt, and other emotions will surface sooner or later. Recognizing each emotional ingredient is most important in overcoming this miserable, often incapacitating illness that is depression. Only when each is recognized can its source be traced and its impact eradicated.

In this section we'll be looking at different age groups affected by depression. Some chapters will be addressed to parents; others will be addressed to adults who may be suffering.

1

Infants

*H*e *was simply too* good! Ben's clothes were too clean and un-rumpled; his toys were not dented or scratched; and his soft brown hair was too orderly. His big blue eyes were all that seemed alive as he sat quietly in the corner of the sofa watching the other children play. Ben was twelve months old, and only three months earlier, he had been down on the floor squirming his way after the bright red ball, cleaning the floor with his bright yellow rompers, and squealing in delight when he retrieved it.

But now he refused to play; he sat silently—all too clean and frighteningly good. His face gave us a clue to his problem. His blue eyes were alert and focused well on interesting objects, but his face looked constantly sad. Though he did not cry, he impressed those of us who watched as a forlorn child.

Ben's mother, Clara, helped us understand what had produced the change in him. Soon after Ben's birth, his father had changed toward the family. He no longer kissed the three children, he ignored the baby, and he hardly spoke to Clara. When Ben was only nine months old, his father left the family completely.

To support the children, Clara had to go to work. After a long day in her office, she had to keep up the house, do the laundry, and try to help the older children with homework. Ben was so good that it became easy to postpone time with him, and he usually fell asleep by himself.

Gradual Change

His unusually observant baby-sitter noticed the gradual but progressive change in Ben. When she discussed this with Clara, Clara reacted, at first, defensively. She certainly was doing the best she could! And Ben was *so good*. Surely he was okay.

But the days and weeks went by without improvement. Ben could not walk, showed little interest in books or toys, and rarely laughed or cried. The pediatrician could find no physical reason for Ben's sudden cessation of development.

Clara decided to make some changes. She was able to reduce her working time, and she asked for help from a teenage neighbor. She spent much time with Ben, rocked him, sang to him, showed him bright pictures, and tickled his tummy and toes.

Slowly but surely Ben began again to hold his toys and throw his ball. He vaguely smiled at the tickling, and one wonderful day, he laughed out loud. When Clara got down on the floor with him and moved his favorite toy just beyond his reach, he crept toward it. Soon Ben was crawling, and in no time he was walking and beginning to say words. He even cried at times, and to Clara's relief, he acted angry at times, too.

Obviously Ben had suffered from infantile depression. It began with the total loss of a loved one—his father. In quick sequence he partially lost his mother, his sister and brother, and his familiar home surroundings. Clara's grief and her anxiety regarding her ability to "make it" alone had blinded her to his plight. And because of his inborn, compliant temperament, Ben had retreated to a lonely world of "goodness."

If the baby-sitter had failed to notice Ben's unusual behavior, or if Clara had refused to admit the truth, he could have grown to school age appearing to be retarded or even to adulthood with chronic, severe depression.

In infants, unfortunately, few people consider the possibility of depression. And that is not surprising considering the inability of infants to verbalize or to describe their feelings. *The Diagnostic and Statistical Manual of Mental Disorders* says that "for children under six, a dysphoric mood [a loss of interest or pleasure in usual activities and pleasures] may have to be inferred from a persistently sad facial expression."[1]

Depression Caused by Parent-Child Separation

Two types of depression caused by parent-child separation are described in the literature—anaclitic depression and institutionalism. In addition, a third type of depression is a source of growing concern—infant day care.

Anaclitic Depression

Anaclitic depression must be suspected if the following three signs are present. *(a)* The child is unable to respond to attention. Such a child simply stares and does not reach out to the one who is trying to elicit some reaction. *(b)* The child shows a weight loss or at least fails to gain weight and develop. *(c)* The child does not show the normal change in facial expression when one would expect sadness, joy, or frustration. The face and eyes appear strangely waxen and unchanging.

The term *anaclitic* refers to the period in a young child's life when he or she is closely tied to the parent and is still totally dependent on that parent. If prolonged separation from the parent takes place, the baby will feel abandoned and, after a period of anger and crying, will seem to give up in infantile despair.

In anaclitic depression, the recovery is slow. This condition develops in some children as young as five or six months of age when

1. *The Diagnostic and Statistical Manual of Mental Disorders,* 3rd ed. (American Psychiatric Association, 1980), p. 213.

they are separated from their mothers for as short a time as four to six weeks. Even seeing the mother once a week during such separations is not enough to prevent this tragic depression from taking over.

Substituting a warm, loving caretaker for an absent mother can make a difference. It may even prevent serious depression. Interestingly enough, depression is less severe if the mother has been a poor caregiver. Recent studies show that the absence of a mother seems less harmful to an infant if there has never been a period of great closeness or "bonding" between mother and child. A child in this type of situation has so little attachment to lose, there is almost no grief.

Paradoxically, good parenting results in healthy bonding between a mother and baby. When prolonged separation occurs, it creates a sense of loss and grief. Despite the grief and depression, such a child is likely, in the long run, to be more emotionally healthy than one who has never experienced such closeness.

A mother may be separated from her child, perhaps due to illness, or, in today's world, for a variety of personal or professional reasons. The example of Ben and his mother is such a situation. Separation was not total, but it was marked enough to cause the classic signs of anaclitic depression in Ben.

Institutionalism

In the early 1920s, child specialists began to notice problems with young patients who had to be in a hospital for a long time. These patients took a longer time to recover and, in the case of really serious illness, were more likely to die than were infants cared for at home where good care was available. Babies who went through such hospital stays became unable to respond to affection by showing a loving response. In fact, they often became unable to relate to others in any way and would lie all too quietly in their cribs while others would explode in anger. Many of them returned to thumb-sucking or bed-wetting. They often refused to eat and might go back to bottles. Fortunately, within a few days of returning home, such symptoms would disappear.

Don't be worried, however, if your child becomes ill enough to have to enter a hospital. Hospitals no longer shut parents out. When I was in medical training (about three decades ago), most hospitals did exclude parents from spending much time with an ill child because the child would cry and become so upset when parents left that it was feared his recovery would be endangered.

We now know that babies who become upset in such circumstances are simply showing signs of healthy bonding and love with the parents. In fact, we worry when children fail to show grief at parents' leaving, and we understand problems occur when parents are entirely excluded.

Hospitals now go to great lengths to enable parents to stay with a young child as much as possible. They know recovery will occur more rapidly, and the child will be better for it.

Infant Day Care

The need for infant day care has created a new type of parent child separation. Several researchers share a growing concern about the increase in leaving very young infants in day care for extended periods.

In many cases, parents believe they have no other choice. Due to the cost of living or the ever-increasing problem of divorce, parents *must* work, and working parents must have help with care for their children. They find the best care available, but work schedules may necessitate lengthy separations of infants from parents every day.

If this is your predicament, I strongly urge you to seek out a substitute mother who cares for only a very few children in her home. Relating with one person other than parents is not very difficult for almost any child. But coping with a number of different persons every day *is*.

When it is possible for you to remain with your child, I urge you to do so. You may need to lower your economic standards somewhat, but if you can survive for at least the first eighteen months of your child's life without leaving home to work, I believe you will be glad later. Part-time work after this period seems to have little or no ill effect, and after age three, children may even benefit from time in a preschool.

Recently my local city newspaper printed a poignant letter from a caregiver in a day-care center—obviously an excellent one! The writer described the numbers of preschoolers who were left for lengthy periods in her care. She had observed several who habitually looked sad. She described one as an especially wistful youngster. As she tucked the child in bed for a nap, the child clung to her asking hopefully, "Will you be my mommy?"

The worker assessed this child's needs accurately, closing her letter thus: "If a day-care worker, responsible for six or seven youngsters, can be a better mommy than a child's own, what is to become of that child?"

Here are some very optimistic answers to that question.

• Leave your child under the age of three (or at *most* under eighteen months) as little as possible. Live as economically as you can during those crucial months if that will keep both parents from having to work outside the home. The cost of child care is so great that in many cases the added family income is not actually very substantial.

Finding a part-time job when your spouse can take care of your child(ren) is an excellent solution. This plan promotes close ties between children and *both* parents and offers a family a chance for the often *needed* additional income. I warn you, however, to work extra hard at keeping your romance warm and your marriage strong. Knowing that you are a *committed* team can make your sacrifices an offering of unusually satisfying love. Or feeling resentful and self-pitying can destroy your relationship.

• If both of you *must* work, or if you are a single parent and truly have no other choice, plan carefully for excellent child care. Excellence may well be defined as a capable grandmother who could come to your home and offer loving child care to supplement her Social Security income. It may mean that you find a young mother who would fit your child among her own, providing a family atmosphere for your child. It may at times mean a commercial child-care center. If so, be certain that a specific person is assigned to your child consistently; you would do well to spend some time talking with the caregivers to find the one best suited to meet your child's needs.

- During the crucial early years of your child's life, keep your priorities in order. An elegantly kept home and elaborately prepared meals are relatively unimportant. So is an active social calendar or even a too-busy church or business schedule. Your child's trust and security rest in *you!* Keep your time and energy free to enjoy the youngster. Play, laugh, work, and even cry together while your child is little and wants that closeness! All too soon he will be out with his friends and involved in his own interests. You can then pursue your interests without risking your child's emotional health.

- During the time you have with your infant, plan a balance in activities according to your child's age.

   The first three months, your baby mainly needs to eat and sleep. At feeding times, smile and talk gently to the infant. Rocking and snuggling will help your baby feel secure and usually are joys to mom and dad as well! At bath time and whenever you like, allow those tiny fists to grasp your fingers and pull gently. Kisses on head, neck, tummy, and feet will stimulate your baby to feel your nearness and love. (I strongly urge you to avoid stimulating the baby's genital areas since this is a strong feeling babies do not need or understand and could lead to abuse later.) By three to six weeks of age, the infant will probably smile and soon will "coo" or "gurgle" in delight during this gentle playtime.

   Between three and six months the baby will become more and more active and like more play. You may blow on the tummy or into the neck, tickle the toes, and stroke the head. You can expect delighted chortling in response. Talk and sing to your baby. Continue to rock him, and begin to jostle and roll him back and forth from side to side. Maintain lots of smiling and loving eye contact.

   Six to nine months is a most delightful period of an infant's life. At this time the infant loves to be swung in your arms, from high to low and side to side. By now you needn't smile or laugh to make your child laugh. His obvious glee will repay your earlier efforts and will make you laugh in the sheer joy of his delight!

After nine months, your child will be crawling and pulling herself up to explore your entire house. You will need to be certain that it is safe for your new adventuress. And you will need to be very near her at all times to make sure she does not hurt herself.

At this time a new era emerges in the field of discipline and training. As well as protecting your infant by "childproofing" your home, you need to begin to teach self-control by defining certain limits. Teach your child what is allowed and what is forbidden. This instruction demands close observation and firm, decisive action with all the protective love you can muster. Following through at this crucial age will make later stages much more fun for both of you because your child will have learned to respect your authority.

If you must use caregivers apart from yourselves, Parents, be certain they, too, understand these concepts. In that way a consistency will develop to provide security for your youngster's developing personality and avoid setting the stage for later depression.

- Completing the balance in playtime and training with your child is the list of other demands on your daily schedule. Certainly you must meet your personal needs for rest and privacy if you are to find the energy to properly care for your child. When your child is sleeping or reasonably content with toys and individual activities, take care of yourself and find time to be with your spouse.

  I find that children are more likely to find some of their own activities when parents are busy. So have your infant near you as you do laundry or household tasks. Give bits of attention to your child, but do *not* feel that you must devote your total attention during every waking minute.

If you follow these practices, I feel confident that you will have done your best to avoid depressive conditions for your infant.

Depression Caused by Neglect and Abuse

In addition to parent-child separations, two other factors emerge as causes of infant depression—neglect and abuse.

Neglect

Neglect is an area of concern easily overlooked. A baby who is exceptionally good or happens to adapt quickly to situations will often fail to express clearly his needs for attention. Without realizing it parents may neglect such a quiet child, and he may feel abandoned and become depressed.

In today's stress-filled world, parents at times become depressed and anxious. When parents are sad, they find it difficult to smile, they have too little energy to play, and even their voices sound troubled. Children of troubled parents commonly learn to act and feel depressed, too.

Abuse

Abuse is increasing at a horrifying rate. An accurate assessment of the incidence of child abuse is virtually impossible to determine. Estimates (and at best they are only estimates) vary from 750,000 to almost 1.5 million cases annually.[2] Reports of abuse are limited almost entirely to physical abuse or physical neglect. Emotional aspects of parent-child problems are equally damaging, but emotional abuse is difficult to define, much less prove.

So many times, I have seen abused children with their hollow, frightened eyes. Their nervous mannerisms and startled withdrawal over any sudden motion reveal the tragedy of their everyday lives. Parents do not intend to abuse their children, but their own inner stresses are too much and their personal resources are too few. They simply "lose it" and take out on their children the frustrations that are too much for them to manage. Although such abuse is much more common in older children, infants may be victims, too.

2. Paul V. Trad, *Infant and Childhood Depression* (New York: John Wiley & Sons, 1987), pp. 226–227.

Effects of Abuse or Neglect

It is my experience that parents almost always want to be good parents. The sad truth is that they simply do not know how. Because of the deterioration of family unity for the past several decades, many of today's parents did not have the opportunity to grow up in a stable, loving, two-parent family. They experienced grief over losing one parent and neglect while the remaining parent went through grief or became depressed. These children certainly missed out on the role models needed to develop a healthy attitude and that intuitive sense of adult parenting of their own youngsters.

Such relative neglect of the infants born in the 1940s may well have left them without the enriching stimulation that would prepare them to handle their babies in a loving and joyful fashion that sets the basis for a good self-image. Dr. Burton White of Harvard University describes a child's need for his parents not to just *love* him, but to be *in love* with him.

People who are *in* love are preoccupied with the object of their affections. They cannot wait to be with him, want to touch him, and share his every feeling and thought. Child specialists are finding that, instead, many parents unconsciously try to avoid their child's presence and know very little about what to do with the baby they have created. One clinic has developed a program to teach parents how to play with their infants.

We have known for many years that infants need to play an active role in the development of the healthy bonds of intimacy between them and their parents. A baby whose every need is anticipated, and who never gets to cry, will very probably grow into a child who expects constant attention and an adult who is overly demanding, in both the home and the workplace. At the other extreme, a baby who is allowed to cry to the point of exhaustion before needs are met is likely to become an excessively aggressive adult or an apathetic one who gives up and develops a what's-the-use? attitude.

In the healthy center of those extremes are the parents who dearly love and value each other and themselves. They will allow their infant to fuss and cry a little before they offer their presence and decipher her needs. They do not hover or neglect, and as this fortunate child grows, she figures life out pretty accurately. "Let your needs be known, and some nice, caring person, sooner or later, will help you out." She will assert herself, but she can postpone gratification because she trusts the needs to be met in a reasonable time and in a loving way.

Remember that depression is composed of pain, anger, helplessness, fear, and sometimes guilt and hopelessness. Surely, then, you can see the predicament of the neglected infant and the certainty with which the individual faces depression in life. The hungry or lonely child, with the physical and emotional pain these states involve, is helpless except for his ability to cry. When there is no response to crying, he experiences frustration and hopelessness. The fear of abandonment reaches horrifying levels, and the neglected child is certain to be depressed.

Few children are totally neglected, so the confusion resulting from not knowing if anyone will respond or what sort of treatment will be forthcoming will create a neurotic pattern. If the parent who finally comes to his aid is reasonably pleasant, a baby will usually react with some delight and affection and will do his part to forge a loving bond with that parent. However, if the parent is grouchy or rough or if the baby was born with a passive temperament, he is less likely to show loving appreciation and may withdraw in fear.

Parents, wanting to be good, will certainly feel they are bad when their infant reacts negatively or even indifferently to them. Such ineffective, but well-intentioned parents almost always endured disappointing treatment when they themselves were children. And they deeply yearn for the loving responsiveness from their child that they rarely received from their parents.

When a baby does not respond lovingly, parents may feel a renewal of the early rejection they experienced with their own parents. These are *feelings,* not thoughts, however. They are almost entirely unconscious, but the needs they recall may result in damaging reactions. Powerless in childhood to communicate to their parents the pain they felt at being neglected or abused, these individuals in adulthood may explode. They can no longer keep that old childish rage bottled up, and they take out on the helpless baby the frustrations of their own childhood.

The Abusive or Neglectful Parent

If you are an abusive or neglectful parent, you are almost certain to be suffering from depression because of your early life experiences. You may be quite successful in every other area of your life, but in your family relationships you were not given the proper tools with which to work. You must be aware, then, of double jeopardy—your early deprivation and pain and the risk of reinflicting these on your child.

Such family problems are relatively common. I suspect in some degree they affect at least half of American families. In some studies fully one-fourth of the families admitted they could abuse a child. I'm certain an equal number have just not recognized the possibility in themselves, or they haven't the courage to admit it.

If you are an abusing parent or feel out of control with your child even occasionally, *do seek help!* Many communities have a chapter of Parents Anonymous for parents who have been child abusers. The staff of your local department of child welfare will be only too happy to help you or direct you to help. Any good family counselor can help you and your family to work together to overcome such actions. And remember, the heavenly Father loves both you and your child. In prayer, seek His wisdom, love, and power to become the parent you want to be.

When we review the broad social and cultural events that have taken place over the past five decades, we should not be surprised at the epidemic of depression in the 1990s. It could hardly be otherwise since the hurts, anger, helplessness, fear, and hidden guilt of repeated generations have accumulated and taken their toll.

Your generation can be the turning point. If you will take the trouble to understand depression, find the honesty to face it in yourself, and acquire the courage to battle it, you can win. There are excellent resources for help, so daring to admit your need and then working with your helper can indeed free you. You can then raise your children to know your love and acceptance, to be secure in the knowledge of their worth, and to develop the healthy self-esteem that reflects being created in the very image of God.

Questions to Help Parents Take Stock

Here are some questions to help you take stock. Are you being the sort of parents who may have a depressed child or a healthy one?

- Are you pleased to be a parent most of the time?

- Would you like more time with your baby?

- Do you enjoy nursing or otherwise feeding your child?

- Do you find yourself instinctively watching out for your infant's safety and well-being?

- Do you look forward to playing and interacting with your child? Does playtime end up happily for both of you?

- Are you willing to forgo long periods (over one or two days until your baby is nearly three) away from your baby?

- If your baby has to be in a hospital, are you willing to spend a great deal of time there? (Guided, of course, by your doctor.)

- Do you have realistic dreams and wishes for your baby? Are you willing to modify these to fit the infant's developing possibilities?

- In discipline, are you able to avoid harshness that could leave physical or emotional scars?

- Are you proud of something in your child and his daily activities? Do you tell him and others about it frequently?

If you have answered yes to most of these questions, the chances are very good that your infant will not become seriously depressed and will develop a sound foundation of healthy self-esteem!

SIGNS AND SYMPTOMS

Depression in Infants

1. *Facial expression.* Depressed infants look sad or at least somber. Over a period of time, however, they may simply appear expressionless.

   Be careful to distinguish the occasional children who seem to be unusually intelligent. They look "thoughtful" and smile only rarely. They thrive, are curious, and are quite normal.

2. *Activity level.* Depressed infants usually go through an early period of excessive crying and restlessness, but eventually they become withdrawn and tend to lie or sit still for long times.

3. *Responsiveness.* At least by three months, normal infants smile and respond to a friendly adult with rapid motion of their legs and arms as if trying to get to the person they see. Depressed infants fail to do so. They lie passively, unsmiling, as if they do not see the onlooker.

4. *Failure to thrive.* Depressed infants may eat fairly well, but they fail to gain weight, do not develop motor skills, and become passive emotionally. In severe cases, infants may seem retarded or act as if they cannot hear.

2

*Toddlers
and
Preschoolers*

*B*y *the time* a child reaches age two or three, depression may look quite different from that in an infant, that is, unless it has continued without improvement from an earlier age. Toddlers and preschoolers often mask their depression with hyperactivity or even aggression. The mechanism is illustrated by a true story a young grandfather told me. He and his son had been working on their house, and he had fallen from a ladder. The fall temporarily immobilized him, and he was in severe pain. His two-year-old grandson, Rusty, playing nearby, approached him looking anxious, but then Rusty kicked him in the face! His pain was even more intense until he could finally call for help.

As we retraced that event, we both agreed that the two-year-old, usually a happy, well-disciplined child, had not suddenly become a monster. He was frightened and desperately wanted to make his grandpa move and become all right again. The behavior of this anxious two-year-old is similar to that of children who are truly depressed. The events that cause depression in toddlers are always frightening, and their aggressive behavior is their attempt to accumulate enough power to neutralize that fear.

Billy's story is a classic example of a truly depressed toddler. Two-year-old Billy's mournful blue eyes focused with deep yearning on his mother and baby brother. She was nursing the new baby, looking tenderly at the perfection of his tiny body. Just three weeks ago Billy had been the recipient of that love and had nursed that same breast. Now he had to stand aside, lonely, rejected, and depressed.

At last his mother noticed him and was moved with some compassion for his feelings. As soon as possible, she put the baby to bed and picked up her displaced older son. She realized that she had been nursing him regularly only the day before she had given birth to the baby. Billy was still only a baby, and his mother knew that he must feel sad over the loss of her time and attention.

Billy's mother picked him up and cuddled him. He nuzzled her, obviously seeking access to her breast—the source of his earlier nurture and comfort. Believing she would meet his needs and relieve his jealousy by nursing him, too, his mother offered him the chance to nurse as he had always done.

Billy, faced with intense ambivalence, began his familiar practice of nursing. He wanted to be the sole focus of his mother's attention, and he was angry that she seemed to prefer the baby to him. Unable to clearly focus his thoughts, much less verbalize them, Billy acted out his frustration. He bit his mother's nipple so hard that it was half severed from the breast.

Billy's father worked very hard, putting in long hours. He rarely found time for his son and was a morose and often angry man who frightened his child. When his mother shared the attention he once had monopolized, Billy could not tolerate the abandonment. He became angry, then sad and fearful. He recalls feeling guilty about hurting his mother but desperate for her attention.

Even now, his personality bears the marks of the depression that became lifelong. Billy is now Bill, a man of middle age who is serving a term of some five years in prison. His mother wears the scars of his angry attack on her breast, but the scars that became etched in his life are even more indelible and far more damaging.

By three or four years of age, children have an uncanny sensitivity to their parents. Watching them play with dolls makes this fact extremely clear. They will treat their dolls precisely as they perceive their parents have handled them. I have watched children spank dolls with intensity, and I have seen those same children, with equal feeling, love, comfort, and protect those dolls.

If you ever want some information on the sort of parent you have been, watch your preschoolers play with a baby doll. The interactions will be a bit exaggerated, just as a good cartoonist exaggerates distinguishing physical features in her art. But all the more clearly, if you will, you can see your own strengths and weaknesses.

By and large, the way little children feel is exactly the way they act. A notable exception to this rule of thumb is in the area of depression. Worry, grief, and anxiety, which are closely interwoven with depression, also may be exceptions.

Let me give you an example. Anne, a young mother of a vivacious three-year-old son, sat in my office on a warm summer day. She had been unable to find anyone to care for Sean, and she desperately needed her counseling session, so she brought him along with some activities to occupy his energy.

Anne was suffering from a very painful experience—her husband was having an affair. As she discussed her pain at feeling less than the other woman, her eyes rained tears, and at times her slender young shoulders shook with silent sobs. Anne was speaking softly and trying to hide her deeply anguished emotions from her young son. She was, however, so preoccupied with her own pain that she failed to observe his quizzical looks.

At last Sean could sit still and color no longer. He came to Anne and patted her arm in a gesture of tender love. Absentmindedly, she touched him and suggested he go back to his crayons.

But Sean could no longer be distracted with coloring balloons and clowns. His face became tense, and his blue eyes filled with fear. His body wriggled and squirmed under the burden of his concerns. If Mom was this upset, who could help him? What really was wrong? He knew Dad was gone a lot, but Sean was accustomed to his being at work. Was something wrong with both Dad and Mom? He'd just have to do something about that. (At least these are my interpretations of Sean's thoughts.)

My attention was distracted by Sean's needs as I listened to

Anne's distress. He began to scribble with his black crayon. Soon he tore out a page from his coloring book, crumpled it, and threw it at me—perhaps the safest target at the moment. Then he began to walk around the room and look out the window. He was obviously searching for either a refuge or a target.

Fortunately, he was willing to sit in my grandmotherly lap and listen as I attempted to reassure him. I explained, simply and softly, that his mother was sad right now. Later on she would explain to him what that sadness was all about. I assured him that she was going to be okay again, but there would be lots of times when she might cry or be upset in the next few weeks just as he became upset over a playmate who broke his toy or wouldn't take turns. I asked him if he became worried or scared to tell his mother, and she would take care of him. All of us, even grown-ups, I explained, have sad times, and that's when we need others to love and help us. So he could love and comfort Mom, and she would also help him. Sean looked at me a moment and then returned to his activities.

Such behavior in children is another mirror for adults. Children do one of two things when they experience grief or depression: (1) they attempt to evade it through excessive activity (Sean's pacing about), or (2) they deny their vulnerability through acting angry or aggressive (Sean's scribbling and tearing of his coloring book). Many adults behave this way, too. They deny their depression by acting strong or even gruff, or they avoid it through feverish activities.

Let me explain that grief and depression are nearly identical in young children. Grief is a response to loss that includes sadness and fear, is often disguised by anger, and is complicated by feelings of guilt. It occurs when children are truly helpless to deal with either the loss or their response.

Depression in childhood results from a series of losses without a completion of the grief process. Grieving includes denial of the loss, anger when it is recognized, preoccupation with the hurts involved, and, usually, resignation and healing. When a child does not receive explanations, a listening ear, caring, and comfort, the grief is not resolved and healing cannot take place. Such a child will almost certainly become depressed.

In preschoolers as in toddlers, the ability to think abstractly is very poor. They see, react, and think directly and simply. Seeing Anne's tears first caused Sean to try comfort. When that failed to dry her tears, he acted out his worry by scribbling and tearing the book. He may not have power over Mom's tears, but he had control over the paper and crayons. When even that was not enough to reassure him, he used his whole body to react to his mounting concerns.

Unfortunately, Sean's situation was not rare. What if I had not been there or had not understood his behaviors and interpreted his anxious emotions? His mother was immersed in her grief and anxiety. Her best attempt to reassure him was totally inadequate and even added to his concern because it was different from her usual careful parenting.

What happens to a majority of children who experience loss and grief is some degree of isolation. They must turn to their own devices. Instinctively, they mourn over a missing daddy; intuitively, they attempt to comfort a grieving mommy. But when no one helps them give direct expression to their feelings, the feelings subside after awhile. And then traumatized children will build a layer of shell-like protection about themselves. They will not reach out too much to adults; they will stay a bit angry or withdrawn and will learn to hide their true feelings with busyness or a rude sort of anger.

Over the weeks, losses in preschoolers will result in grief with its denial, anger, sadness, guilt, and fear. Over the months, how these losses are perceived and how the grief is comforted will determine much of each child's future mental health and emotional stability. There are four options to deal with these problems.

1. Even offering brief, simple interpretations (such as mine with Sean) can bring reassurance and a sense of security. That things are tough now but will get better is a believable truth.

2. Covering up the problem seems tempting. So many parents attempt to act as if everything is as usual. Let me assure you, kids won't be fooled, and what they imagine is often worse than the truth.

3. Being overprotective is easy to do. The parent may tell the child about a problem and then sympathize too much, unwittingly allowing the child to react with self-pity.

4. Explaining the problem but refusing the permission to express feelings is another possibility. Anne demonstrated to Sean her way to deal with hurts—tears and talking. She reported that his father, on the other hand, allowed no expression of emotion. If Sean cried, he was told to be tough or to go to his room.

A number of studies reveal a link between unsatisfactory parent-child relationships and depression in adult life.[1] It is therefore extremely important to establish a loving, healthy relationship with your child. This relationship will be characterized by the following:

- *Honesty* is needed the most. Without it nothing else (even love) is believable.

- *Openness*—simple, clear explanations of problems and interpretations of parents' feelings, actions, and decisions—will do much to prevent a child's grim fantasies.

- *Good judgment* regarding when and how much to tell a child is vital. Do not describe all the painful details of a relative's death from cancer or all the reasons for an upcoming divorce.

- *Genuine caring* for the child is evident by avoiding both overprotectiveness and denial of the problems.

- *Effective communication* is also essential to deal with the events of life. You listen to each other with your minds and hearts, you establish eye contact in order to read the feelings words may not convey, and you take time to be sure you are hearing each other correctly.

1. Daniel J. Burbach and Charles M. Borduin, "Parent-Child Relations and the Etiology of Depression," *Clinical Psychology Review*, vol. 6, 1986, pp. 133–153.

It is relatively easy for you to establish a healthy relationship with your child when she is two to five years old. Through accomplishing this, you can successfully guide her through her childish losses and grief. And this early guidance will prevent most serious depression later on.

Four-Year-Olds

During this year of life, a distinctive habit shows up in most children. That is why I have chosen to comment specifically about them. They become preoccupied with asking questions. "Why did Collie die?" "Did he go to heaven?" "Why?" "Will I die?" "What does God look like?" "Why didn't He answer me when I called His name?"

At no other time in an individual's life is there such a focus on the hows, whys, and whats about those mysterious, supernatural aspects of life. If, during this time, children suffer losses, and experience grief, they may progress to depression. Their questions are no longer remote ones that imply idle curiosity, but are deeply personal ones. Unless someone hears out the questioning, interprets and comforts the feelings, and supplies some answers (no one has answers to *all* of a child's questions!), a child will be left afraid and confused.

At four, depressed children go through some of the aggressive or angry behaviors of two- and three-year olds, and they may revert to more "babyish" actions, such as wetting the bed or thumb-sucking, than would be typical of their age group. But four-year-olds are more likely to weep and much more likely to discuss the events that have caused their depression than are younger children. Sleeping disturbances are common, and the appetite may decrease.

In spite of the obvious helplessness of young children, they have a strange sense of power. Their world revolves largely around them, and they often feel that they are somewhat responsible for things that happen. A four-year-old is likely to believe that his naughtiness causes his mother's headache (and so it may!) or that his refusal to sit on his grandpa's lap somehow caused his heart attack (which it did *not!*).

Four-year-olds have a big, new world facing them soon. They will begin school when they turn five, and they have some sense of the separations and changes that will be involved. From then on, a great many changes and increasing responsibilities will claim their time and energy. If their early childhood foundations are faulty, they will be more vulnerable to both emotional and behavioral problems.

It is essential that parents take time to answer those endless questions, reassure the childish worries, and provide the consistent love four-year-olds need. These efforts will result in strong foundations much less vulnerable to the eroding force of depression.

The Abused Child

Never can I recall such sad, frightened eyes on such a young child. Four-year-old Danny sat among an array of toys. His face rarely broke out of the mold that had cast its mark there over his few brief years of life. Danny could not be enticed to play with the blocks, talk through the puppets, or pretend to make a telephone call. He just sat looking mournfully out of the prison of his large brown eyes. If I moved too suddenly, he winced and moved away. He totally rejected my invitation to sit beside me to share a storybook. Suddenly, without warning, Danny grabbed a bright red block and threw it at me.

Danny demonstrates the classic signs of serious child abuse: a sad facial expression, refusal to play with toys, withdrawal from me (and most adults), unusual response when startled, and unpredictable anger. In fact, he had been abused by both parents.

His mother was depressed and had been abused as a child. She married a man who had the same hasty temper she had become accustomed to in her father. Her abuse of Danny was mainly limited to yelling, threatening, and name calling. Dad, on the other hand, seemed to feel it was good training to grab Danny, shake him, and then throw him into a chair. He slapped the boy frequently, not recognizing his strength when he was angry.

The making of threats of violence by one parent can become just as terrifying to a child like Danny as the acting out of the violence. At least when the physical abuse took place, Danny could relax until the next bout. With his mother's threats, however, he could only wait in silent terror for the blow to fall.

The reported cases of child abuse continue to rise (either because of a distinct increase, as I believe, or because people are at last reporting them more quickly) as does the number of potentially abusive families. One researcher has concluded that about 25 percent of American families could, by their own admission, be abusive. That would mean roughly forty million American children are at risk of being abused.[2]

A well-known fact about abusive parents is that a very high percentage of them were abused as children. It takes no complex computer to reveal the concern we all must share about the generations to come. If some forty million abused children grow up to abuse their children (or even half that many), it is clear that child abuse will grow exponentially!

Each of us must assume it is a personal duty to campaign against abuse. Churches and schools need to teach parents how to train and discipline children effectively and lovingly without abusing them.

If you have been, or recognize that you could be, an abuser of your child, seek help from your minister, a trusted friend, or a professional family counselor. Explain your concern and ask for help *before* you damage your child. Another resource for you is Parents Anonymous. This group is composed of parents who have overcome habit patterns of abuse and are now able to help others achieve success.

I realize there is a risk in seeking this help because some well-meaning people may report you to a child protective agency. The law requires such reporting, and if there is evidence of abuse, the authorities are required to remove children who are at risk from parents. If you seek help and cooperate with that help, this danger is greatly decreased. I trust you will be able to conquer the problem quickly so your children will not be damaged and your family will remain intact.

2. Paul V. Trad, *Infant and Childhood Depression* (New York: John Wiley & Sons, 1987), p. 227.

I most strongly urge you to get help if you are tempted to abuse only one child and you don't understand why. My experience has taught me that selective abuse is due to a hidden resemblance in that child to someone who caused difficulty for the parent. It is, of course, beneficial to uncover such a situation, resolve the old emotions connected to that person, and learn to forgive him. You will then be free from the pain of those old memories and free to establish a comfortable, loving relationship with your child.

It is far better to prevent the depression of an abused child than to have to seek means of relieving it. But if your child (or another child you know) suffers in this way, let me give you some recommendations.

1. Immediately meet with a trustworthy family therapist. If you have abused your child even occasionally for several years, you have a habit that is likely to increase as your child grows older and learns to feed into your feelings, attitudes, and actions. You must learn how to overcome this habit.

2. Find someone who will encourage you, perhaps your spouse, but more likely a reliable friend, a pastor, or a relative. I say "more likely" because spouses often feed into each other's abuse habits. For example, one may report a child's misdeeds to the other who then overdisciplines in an abusive manner.

3. When you find the insight and strength to do so, explain to your child that you have come to realize that you have been too hard on her. Promise that you have stopped the harsh punishment and that you will adopt whatever disciplinary measures you and your counselor believe will teach the needed lesson to your child.

4. Make friends with your depressed and frightened child. You will become aware of his nervousness and startled reaction when you suddenly reach out for him. Because I know you love your child, you will be extremely sad to realize you have hurt him so much. But don't go to the other extreme and pamper him by

trying to "make it up" to him. Just remind him you are sorry for your past bad habits, and then be glad you have changed and can really love your child.

5. Develop a pattern of deliberateness—slow down in your reacting to your child; think about what she has really done and why she did it. Maybe she was nervous and tense instead of deliberately careless. Many children learn early in life to cover fear and worry with hyperactivity and even aggressiveness. Think carefully about what *she* needs more than how *you* feel.

6. What do you want him to learn? That you are powerful and aggressive? Or that you are wise and loving and can teach him to master whatever skills he needs to make it in life?

7. Learn to speak gently, touch lovingly, laugh and play together happily, and learn together how to be a loving, healthy parent and child.

The Neglected Child

I know what I am going to say in this section will put me on the line. Our society is quite divided and *very* emphatic on both extremes regarding the issue of early child care or preschools. Only this week I received a letter from a mother who asked, "Must I send my three-year-old son to preschool? My friends are telling me he won't be ready for kindergarten if I don't send him. But I enjoy having him at home, and he seems so little to have to go away to school."

What a sad letter from a mom who loves her son and wants to be the one to teach him about life! You may be certain that I asked her to listen to her heart. Raising a confident child demands saturating that child with the joy and security of parents who are *in love* with him and who crave time with him. The concept of *needing* to enter preschoolers in academic settings is in most cases erroneous, according to my experience and information.

The other side of this debate relates to the many young children of single-parent homes or those families who, for various reasons, are unable to provide the healthy, stimulating environment children need. Many of these families are in every community, but especially in metropolitan areas. In my opinion, it is a sad commentary on any society if children receive more love and attention from a succession of caregivers in a center than from their own loving parents at home.

A recent issue of *Time* magazine featured two articles on child care outside the home. The magazine noted that in 1986, nine million preschoolers spent their days in the hands of someone other than their mothers. The percentage of mothers of children under six who work outside the home has increased almost threefold, from 19 percent in 1960 to 55 percent in 1986.[3]

The findings of child psychologists have varied over the years. In the late sixties and early seventies when the women's liberation movement mushroomed, several studies seemed to indicate that day care would be perfectly fine for children. At the present time, however, a number of extremely careful researchers in top-rated universities are reversing that opinion. Several noted child psychologists have written and spoken emphatically about their immense concern for youngsters who are separated before the age of three for extensive periods from their parents. (You'll remember that I discussed this earlier in the book.) Other authorities state that current studies are more likely to verify the early research of the fifties than the more superficial findings of the period cited above. At that time (the fifties), the evidence showed that babies could adjust well to *one* regular caretaker besides parents—but not to a succession of strangers.

I suggest you visit several large day-care centers as I have done. I fear you will share my concern at seeing the numbers of sad-eyed children there. I notice caretakers whose attitude is one of obvious indifference to me as a visitor and to the moving mass of little bodies that seem to merge into a blur of miniature humans. I see some children who look puzzled, worried, sad, and angry. Of

3. "The Child-Care Dilemma," *Time,* June 22, 1987, pp. 54–63.

course, many others play happily and seem to adjust well. It may be a good idea to imagine yourself in the place of a helpless child. You may gain unusual insight.

Recently, in a seminar I shared my concerns about children being separated too much from parents, and I encountered responses of intense anger. A number of parents there had to work to support their children and felt I was trying to make them feel guilty. That is not true since I have always worked and I am acutely aware that many working moms—single or married—have no choice.

Let me try to put in order some philosophies that can help you sort through your feelings about your toddler or preschooler—and, I hope, can prevent depression in them or, if need be, remedy it.

1. Think very carefully about your decision to work outside the home. Could you avoid doing this if you lowered your economic level a bit? Having grown up during the Great Depression of the 1930s, I know what we can get along without! We have enjoyed more than three decades of relative affluence in the United States. Perhaps you, too, have learned to live a bit more luxuriously than you need to. You may find it would not be as profitable to go to work as you thought. Just consider it.

2. I know many of you, after profound thought and careful financial figuring, will find you simply cannot make it without both parents' income. If you are a single parent, I know very well you have no choice—at least in most cases.

3. A few women truly cannot tolerate the confinement of staying at home all the time and taking care of children. I've known a few moms who were close to abusing their loved children out of sheer personal frustrations. These women can be reasonably good parents if they are away part-time.

4. In an increasing number of young families, fathers may choose to spend more time with children and less on a job while mothers go to work more. If this plan suits you, I would not

argue against it. However, some fathers who have tried to assume this role eventually rejected it because they felt it destroyed their masculine image.

If your decision clearly demands that you both, or you single parents, go to work, think about these suggestions:

1. Work as near your home for as few hours daily as possible. Try to allow enough time in the mornings and evenings to avoid the rushing that can promote irritability and result in your striking out, verbally or physically, at your child. If the truth could be known, I suspect that parental impatience and grouchiness are worse for a young child than separation.

2. Plan your daily and weekly schedules so you simplify your duties at home as much as possible. Quick cleaning procedures, simple meals, and restricted time on the phone or in front of the TV can free much time to spend with your child.

3. Learn how to have fun with your child. If you truly do not know what she enjoys, observe other families, read books, and ask your minister, relatives, and friends what activities they share with their children. Try out a variety of things such as taking walks to observe nature and people, visiting your public library and checking out children's books, building with blocks, playing easy pitch and catch, some gentle wrestling, and dressing up doll families. Each of these will teach you as much as your child and will strengthen the bonds between you. Have your child "help" you as you work. It will take a bit longer, but she loves to copy your activities now. Later on, she will avoid work unless you can make it a fun, loving activity to share now.

4. A child needs some time to do his own thing. It is not wise to spend every spare minute entertaining him; you could create a tyrant who demands servitude from everyone. Just include him in your usual family and household patterns, and then schedule some special time with him every day. Look at him and listen

when you talk together and respond to him in a naturally loving way. Treat him as you would want to be treated if you were his age.

If Your Toddler or Preschooler Is Depressed

In discussing the depression of the abused child I offered some ideas to relieve that sadness. Those ideas are useful for any depressed child. In addition, let me give you the following suggestions:

- *Search your heart and mind for any hidden resentments* involving this child. Carefully and prayerfully seek to understand why you feel them. Relinquish them to God; He will know just what to do with them. Trust Him to fill you with unconditional love for your child.

- *Find ways every day to express your love* to this sad child. Look at him, touch him—gently, playfully, *appropriately*—listen and respond to him. Correct him lovingly, but firmly and clearly.

- *Be predictable*. In similar situations, learn to react in the same way every time. By that I mean, if you need to correct your child for disobedience, you should do so *every* time she doesn't obey you. Your inconsistency can worry and even frighten her. When she does pick up her toys, compliment her, and express your appreciation every time. Avoid taking good behaviors for granted.

- *Develop a sense of humor*. All of us can make it through difficult days if we can find the fun that exists in most situations, even the worst ones. Be careful to avoid laughing *at* your child, but do introduce laughter *with* him. It is impossible for someone who laughs with regularity to stay depressed.

I trust you have read this in time to avoid having a depressed toddler or preschooler. If not, however, do not despair or become depressed. Just practice love and laughter, and that depression will vanish!

Depression in Toddlers and Preschoolers

1. *Stop, look, and listen*. They behave first in a carefully observant manner, watching the adults around them and listening to conversations.

2. *Run for safety*. At the first sign of sadness or anxiety, they run to an adult with whom they feel secure.

3. *Demand attention*. If the adult's presence does not provide them enough reassurance, they act up. Like the examples given here, they may kick, hit, or bite. Often they use toys for expressing their anxiety, sometimes even breaking treasured toys.

4. *Yell for help*. Rather than cry, they are more likely to yell and act angry. How confusing this is to parents who may punish and even spank children at such times! Lots of misbehaviors by children need correction, but a time of worry and anxiety that comes from a loss (such as Billy's) is not the time for discipline.

5. *Regress to security*. Children of this age commonly revert to earlier habits as a sign of depression. They wet the bed, soil their pants, have temper fits, suck their thumbs, and in general return to acting babyish. And how understandable that is! If we could go back to a time of security and total dependency, perhaps some of us would do so at times. Youngsters, so close to that safe era, are unknowingly grasping for such security.

6. *Experience sleep disturbances*. Nightmares are a very common expression of depression. Through dreams, their impressionable minds try to work out the troubling events of their lives. They may have a difficult time getting to sleep due to anxieties about previous dreams. Children of this age who have bad dreams will often awaken and want to crawl in bed with parents. They should *always* be welcomed under such circumstances, comforted tenderly, and then returned to their own bed.

7. *Cry and whine*. In my experience, crying is more likely to result from physical than emotional pain at this age. Nevertheless, toddlers and preschoolers who have a habit of whining or crying will be more likely to show such patterns of behaving when they are depressed.

3

Young Children

In spite of the range of years (ages five through twelve), depression is manifested similarly throughout this time span. Wendy exemplifies some typical signs and symptoms.

At six, Wendy refused to go out and play with her friends. Previously, she could hardly stop such fun to come to meals. She sat around listlessly, uninterested in books, toys, TV, or even cookie baking. Her lively blue-green eyes and freckled face became dull and pale. Her anxious mother could think of no reasons for the changes. Her doctor could find no physical explanation and suggested it was a phase she would outgrow.

I have learned to follow a useful rule that often solves these mysteries: when all else fails, ask! When her mother finally asked why she stayed in the house and looked so sad, Wendy readily replied, "All my friends keep movin' away, and I miss 'em so much! I'm just not gonna make friends anymore, and then I won't feel bad."

Let's investigate the major causes of depression of children in this age group and their responses to it. If Wendy's mother had been aware of some basic facts about depression, she would have more readily recognized its signs in her daughter, and she would have been prepared to help Wendy become once more her fun-loving self.

Failure

"Let's all sit on the story rug now. We're going to hear all about Calvin the Cat who got lost!" Mrs. Smith was a much-loved, experienced teacher of kindergartners. She could make any story come alive with her animated face and expressive voice. The children eagerly left their crayons and papers, scampering to the familiar story corner with its soft carpet. They waited almost breathlessly for today's event in the life of Calvin.

But they waited in vain, and one by one they turned their attention to Catherine. I could tell by their disgusted looks that she had spoiled their fun before. Catherine was deliberately disobeying Mrs. Smith. She climbed onto the piano in a far corner of the big sunny room. At times she would stop to turn and watch for Mrs. Smith's response. I was only an observer, called to try to help a troubled five-year-old.

Mrs. Smith was torn, I could tell, by the need to corral a straying child and her wish to teach the eager students. They won out, and she began her story. I captured Catherine, carrying her to the group and sitting with a protective arm about her. We both joined in the fun of Calvin and his adventures.

What I learned later explained the child's behavior. She had a mild learning disability and had been unable to keep pace with the other children. What they knew to be a *b* she saw as a *d*. When she could not print her letters correctly, the teacher did not give her the coveted smiling face sticker the others received. Day after day, Catherine tried to make those letters correctly, and Mrs. Smith tried equally hard to help her. But again and again, she reversed letters and numbers. And each time she felt more like a failure.

Her parents tried hard to teach her to behave properly and gave much time to their daughter. But overall, they had failed to help her achieve the respect and compliance she needed to adjust in school.

She added to her learning problems the misbehaviors that antagonized her teacher and estranged her from friends.

We learned that Catherine was angry about her failures and sad about her inability to keep up with her classmates. She compensated for her lack of success by gaining attention through her distractions and climbing. Anger, sadness, helplessness, and inadequacy are the major ingredients of depression, and Catherine experienced all of these.

I have observed many similar children. Unable to keep pace with the majority, they fail a little more every day, and they react in one or more of the ways that will be outlined in this chapter.

It is easy to empathize with them. If you were put down at work, if you realized you simply could not put out the quantity or quality of work your fellow workers did, you would probably quit. But children can't quit—and they shouldn't, of course.

It is often up to you, as a parent, to find the solution to this depression. My suggestions are these:

1. Observe your child closely and spend time exploring a variety of interests with him. When you discover an area in which he can excel, help him develop that skill. Show him you are genuinely proud of his ability, and find avenues for him to pursue in sharing it with others.

2. Practice unconditional love for your child. By consistent affection, shared activities, loving eye contact, and effective discipline make her aware every day of how *much* you love her!

3. Help your child understand that everyone is gifted in different areas of life. She may learn the alphabet more slowly than others, but her level of physical coordination exceeds that of others her age. You may need to help her through the grief of being "different" from her peers in some ways if she is to be able to enjoy and feel confident about the skills she does have.

4. Work with your child's teachers to help them understand him, and work with him to develop healthy confidence about his

uniquely special skills. Try, by the way, to help your child develop patience for teachers who are responsible for a number of pupils.

Even through failures, children can learn to grow in maturity, understanding of and compassion for others, and determination to discover some areas in which they *can* succeed.

Losses

As adults, all of us have experienced losses and recognize the grief that accompanies them. I find, however, that many adults fail to identify the losses of childhood. Even when they do understand, they often fail to help a child work through those painful processes of grief because they do not know how.

At eleven, Janice was already developing into a beautiful young woman. Light brown hair and clear blue eyes topped an angry-looking, hard-set mouth. Learning to read faces has been a great asset in my work, and Janice's was easy reading indeed.

I had been asked to see Janice because she was new to school and was not making a good adjustment. Her IQ was almost in the gifted range, but her grades were all *D*'s and *F*'s. She was insolent and downright rude to her teacher and had little to do with her classmates.

Fortunately, Janice was more than eager to discuss the pain that resulted in such apparent anger and rebellion. It took only my gentle comment, "Janice, you look pretty unhappy!" to turn on her tears. As they melted the hardness of her lovely, young face, she told me about herself.

She had lived with loving parents and a brother in a distant city. Their neighborhood was an economically poor one, but it was rich in friends and caring, supportive people. Janice loved her home, her friends, her entire life, and she doted on her worn family of stuffed animals. They had comforted her childish tears, protected her occasional bad dreams at night, and shared countless secrets.

Then the blow fell. But to Janice's parents, it was far from a catastrophe! Her father received a fine promotion. At last he could provide for his family the things he so yearned to give them. He and his wife were jubilant. Of course, they would need to move to a distant city, but that was not really a big problem. His advancement was certainly worth the move.

Eagerly, the parents traveled across the country to find and settle into a lovely new home. They were able to purchase elegant new furnishings and were ecstatic over their good fortune.

As they prepared to move, Janice's mother gleefully discarded all the old furnishings and household equipment. They were truly leaving behind their old, impoverished past! To Janice's horror, her mother demanded she give up her familiar furnishings and, worst of all, her family of bears and bunnies. To Janice, they were as much a part of her as her very skin.

But her mother was not to be moved. They must be given to the local mission for the poor. Since nothing Janice could do or say changed her mother's mind, she stopped communicating. She grew sullen and refused to cry. Her pet-confidants were gone. Her friends were lost to her. No one could possibly understand. She was angry, sad, and helpless, yet she felt guilty because she was so stubbornly set against the parents she had once loved. Janice was truly depressed and felt any efforts to succeed in school were meaningless. Making new friends made her feel disloyal to her old ones. And what if they had to move again? She would just go through more hurt.

Janice's parents and school staff were eager to comfort and help her through her emotional reaction to the losses that had been so tragic to her. They only needed to understand her feelings, but without help she had been unable to find the words to explain.

Often no one recognizes the pain that underlies the angry exterior of children like Janice. Eventually, they forget the real cause of their grief, and that grief becomes the long-drawn-out experience of depression—its taproot buried in the debris of time and new events.

Parent, here are the things you must do to heal or prevent the depression your child may experience due to losses:

1. *Be aware of the changes that inevitably will occur in your child's life and put yourself in your child's place.* How would you feel? Can you recall similar events or times in your childhood? Perhaps you remember all too well how you felt!

   These changes will include friends' moving (or even becoming angry and rejecting), breaking of favorite toys, losing pets, finishing a year of school (and losing an especially loved teacher), losing freedoms and assuming new responsibilities, learning of the divorce of a friend's parents (or fearing yours!), or adjusting to a new baby with the attendant loss of some of your time and attention. Once you understand this concept of loss, grief, and depression, you will probably discover many other losses that are significant to your child.

2. *Teach your child that sadness, a sort of anger, and a sense of pain are normal under these circumstances.* Help him to come to you for hugs, reassurance, and a listening ear when he feels the pain or sadness. For the anger, teach him how to talk it out or work it out through running, hitting a punching bag, or even crying or yelling a bit. It is useful for a lifetime to understand how to express the pain and anger of grief and then to await the often slow but certain arrival of comfort and healing.

3. *Avoid overreacting or overprotecting.* Both children and adults learn the defeating art of self-pity. All losses are accompanied by pain and anger, but it is always possible to recover from these and return to peace and joy.

4. *Never replace a lost pet or broken item with another until your child has recovered from the sadness and pain of its loss.* Prompt replacement may fix in your child's philosophy of life an unrealistic belief. Our pleasure-seeking society has come to think that we should avoid pain and find pleasure at all costs, but nothing could be more damaging to healthy character building. We all *must* face loss, pain, and grief and learn to transcend them. Replacements deny a child the opportunity to grow through these experiences.

5. *Make yourself available as much as you can and offer your child an opportunity to express her needs and feelings.* Do this regularly until you are certain she has completed the grief. This may take only a few hours, or it may last much longer, depending on the child and the type of loss.

Rejection

Psychoanalysis teaches there are two basic fears in life—the fear of engulfment (such as being eaten by a wild animal or being buried alive in an avalanche), and the fear of abandonment. The latter fear is common in children who have experienced the loss of a person in their lives. Losing friends through a family move, a grandparent through death, or a parent through divorce is common in today's world.

Much more common, but also a cause of depression, is the loss of friends' respect and affection. I can vividly recall the humiliation of being the last chosen on one of my school's baseball teams. I was, to put it kindly, a loser in this sport, and to this day, I have little interest in baseball. Fortunately, I was good at spelling, so I compensated for my rejection in one area by being extra good in another.

But what becomes of children who excel in nothing? Experiencing both failure and rejection, they often withdraw in despair, they imagine they could do well if they wanted to (often true!), or they act in obnoxious ways as Catherine did. Whatever their mode of expression, they *all* experience depression.

Tragically, many children who are rejected by peers have also known rejection from their families. Understandably enough, parents have dreams and goals for their children. They want them to be popular and successful in sports and academics, and they would certainly prefer them to be physically attractive.

Few, indeed, are the children who can measure up in all areas. Without their realizing it, parents' disapproval of a child's falling short of their dreams can result in that child's feeling rejected.

Kevin's parents had great expectations of him. From early on, he did not measure up, but with great intensity and diligence they tried to teach him to be all they dreamed he would be. Yet Kevin's temperament and physique meant he never could gain the approval he craved.

By the time he was ready for playmates, he had developed a habit of overreacting. He tried too hard, laughed too loudly, and gave up too readily. His playmates did not know how to get along with him, so they refused to have anything to do with him after a time.

In school, Kevin simply could not fit in. Though he was bright, his grades were poor; despite his yearning for friends, classmates refused to work or play with him; his teachers could not tolerate Kevin's underachievement. He was rejected, lonely, and depressed.

Slowly, Kevin withdrew into a fantasy world. He imagined the friends he could not win and dreamed about the exploits he was too afraid to attempt. He covered his loneliness and depression with nonchalance and even rudeness, but he was too depressed to function.

Lonely, depressed children like Kevin may even erupt in anger and violence against people who have seemed to reject them. But there is hope for them and their families.

What to Do for a Rejected Child

Here are the actions you as parents or teachers need to take to help the Kevins and Kathys in your care.

1. *Search out your own feelings toward the child.* A child like Kevin can become very frustrating. If you have come to resent the child's problems, he may feel that you dislike *him*. In her book *Something More*, Catherine Marshall discussed the steps to becoming free from resentments. By facing up to them, thinking about the reasons surrounding them, and finally choosing to relinquish them to God's care, you can truly be free of defeating attitudes.[1]

1. Catherine Marshall, *Something More* (New York: McGraw-Hill, 1974).

2. *Replace your resentful attitudes with constructive ones.* Once you understand your own and others' unconscious roles in the formation of your child's problems, you will be eager to make amends. Focus on the really great aspects of your child more than his problems, and you are certain to develop proud and loving attitudes to replace your disapproval and resentment.

3. *When you have mastered positive attitudes, reflect them to your child.* This reflection obviously cannot work until your feelings are straight. Like the trick mirrors that distort an image to a short, fat monster or a tall, skeletal caricature, you will feed your child's problem as long as you have disturbed attitudes. And just as a "true" mirror reflects an exact image, so your balanced and positive feelings and concepts of your child will show him the assets he has. With a valid sense of his strengths, he can successfully solve the problems he has—with your help.

4. *Avoid prolonged worry about your child.* I doubt that any good parent can avoid worry all the time. But when your face and actions reflect undue concern for days at a time, your child will get the message that she is a problem. And she will feel hopeless or become defiant and rebellious. If you have cause for concern, define the problem, solve it, and resume enjoying your child. If you need help with the problem, seek it promptly, work with your helper (a counselor, friend, or clergy member), and then get on with a better life.

5. *Develop a warm, trusting, happy relationship with your child.* Positive peer relations have their foundations in healthy family relations. As you find your child worthy of your friendship, he will learn gradually to form comfortable relationships with peers. And no one who genuinely loves and is loved by family and friends can stay depressed.

6. *Teach your child to be friendly—with herself and others.* Remember that Jesus Christ said, "Love the LORD your God . . . [and] your neighbor *as yourself*" (Matthew 22:37, 39, emphasis

added). If you are not certain of your child's feelings about herself, observe the peers to whom she turns. We all gravitate to people with whom we have the most in common. As you teach your child to love herself, as you learn to love her unconditionally, she will find friends who also are loving. What a remarkable cure for rejection!

7. *Back up and start over.* If your child is five or six, you can more easily correct the damaging impact of too much disapproval and rejection. If your child is older, you may need to revert mentally to the time when you began to worry about and feel strong displeasure with him. In that case, discuss your mistakes, apologize, and change your attitudes. Start, emotionally, at that period of your child's development, and reparent him. Avoid any condescending attitude; don't treat him like a baby. But practice the patient explaining, and loving reassurance that you would have used at that time—had you known you needed to do so.

Social Misfit

My ancestors were all a part of the culture of the "plain people." From every branch of my family tree I can find only those stern, almost forbidding people dressed uniformly in blacks, browns, or dark blues who lived by a strict set of rules.

As an adult, I cherish the values and strength of character they gave me by their consistent examples. I treasure their individuality (despite their outer conformity), their courage to stand for their values in a permissive world, and their limitless compassion and outreach to those in need.

Yet as a child I chafed and even suffered under the regulations that made me so different from my peers. My clothes were of bright colors and often attractive designs, but my sleeves were long, and I never wore ankle socks until my "rebellious" teen years. I was not allowed to go to a skating rink or a circus; movies and dancing were not even discussed; and my language was so clean it was stilted! I felt almost totally a misfit among friends in school and even in a church with beliefs less strict than those of my parents.

New clothes came to be a heartache rather than a joy as I wept in futility over a sleeve length that could *not* be "just one inch shorter." My helplessness, my anger at what seemed to me irrational rigidity, and my painful sense of "differentness" combined to leave me depressed many times.

Fortunately, I had many good times with my family, and their love and devotion to me and one another countered this one area of pain with many benefits. My good mind and the sensitivity to others' needs and feelings eventually won for me many lasting friendships.

But what about Brenda? She was a child in the early part of the 1970s. Her long skinny legs never felt relaxed under too-short, hand-me-down clothes from neighbors. Her dresses never "fit"—in length or in style and color. Her fine, straight hair refused to stay in the unfashionable style her mother chose.

Brenda was immature and used "baby talk" far too long. She was overprotected and never learned to stand up for herself. Painfully self-conscious and so aware of never fitting in, Brenda could not even study effectively. Both her teachers and her parents believed her to be a slow learner, if not actually retarded. At home, she was treated like a child and mercilessly teased by her siblings. She could find not a single good thing about herself.

Those years of being a social misfit took their toll in personal misery with prolonged depression. Later she alleviated this pain by using chemicals that brought her temporary "highs."

Solemn blue eyes peered doubtfully at me through gold-rimmed glasses. Robert's blond hair was cut short and neatly parted. His knit shirt was too pressed and clean, and his manner was stiff. Most boys wore jeans, thin at the knees, but Robert's corduroys were new and smartly creased.

I had been asked to see Robert because he was an underachiever—a child who was intellectually gifted but was making barely passing grades. He was a loner, rarely smiled, and seemed to find no friends.

It was certainly clear to Robert that his problem was his parents. He hated the clothes they made him wear, the frequent haircuts they demanded and, worst of all, the fact that they refused to permit a television set in their home. While the other children laughed about last night's comedy or the latest episode of "Masters of the Universe," he sat in stony silence. He knew nothing about their interests. My empathy for Robert was profound. I, too, had been a misfit because of my parents' excessive strictness.

Whether the cause is poverty or affluence, well-meant strictness in values or simply ignorance of children's needs, being too different can result in depression and even despair in a child. The cure for being different sounds simple, but it may be most difficult. It almost always has its taproot in the parents' childhoods. Their beliefs in a certain constricted life-style are bound by a buried fear of disaster of some sort if they should permit changes.

My mother really feared I might become a rebellious, immoral adult if she allowed me to dress and act in a mode that fit my peers. Her strictness, I was to learn later, was prompted by her protective love for me.

Brenda's parents did not consider stylish clothes to be important. They failed to realize the painful differentness she experienced. And they never understood the depression she developed or the temptations she faced to escape through addiction.

And Robert's parents were, like mine, so afraid of his becoming a ruffian, even learning violence from TV, that they were trying to fit him into a mold of total respectability.

These parents failed to change; their own rigid upbringing and the fear that was woven into the very fiber of their beings were too strong.

But you can be different. You can change. Here's how.

1. *Remember your own childhood and how badly you felt* at your parents' *unnecessary* strictness.

2. *Learn to collect facts and to separate valid information from old fears.* Allowing me to wear at least moderately stylish clothes would have increased my social confidence, would have prevented years of painful shyness, and would have enabled me to reach out to others in positive ways. If Robert's parents had

allowed him to wear nice jeans, he would have felt more comfortable, and he would not have been a "slob." And if they had taught him how to watch TV with discretion and selectivity, he could have discussed good programs with friends. He may even have influenced some of them to select better TV viewing.

3. *Find that increasingly rare balance in the necessary limit setting* that provides security for children and the freedom to choose that teaches them healthy responsibility.

Guilt

Even the lights in the classroom could not dispel the gloom of the stormy March day. And my concern seemed equally ineffective in reaching through the cloud of anger that hung over Tim.

He was restless, moving from chair to chair, even leapfrogging over them. Despite his constant motion, Tim revealed many facts to me. His set jaws and flashing eyes allowed me to feel the anger that bristled in his words and voice. His once happy family had been shredded by alcoholism. Only a few months earlier his parents had separated, and he had bravely chosen to live with his mom, by then a severe alcoholic. Tim was worried about her—she spent most of the time in bed, had stopped cooking and keeping house, and was grouchy. She often had boyfriends in, and then she would dress up and act happy.

Tim was afraid to return to his father who was holding together the rest of the family in a fairly happy home. Tim's fear was profound. If he left his mom, she could die; she might never eat; her cigarettes could cause a fire; one of her "friends" could hurt her.

Furthermore, ten-year-old Tim was not a match for all the tasks that were required to keep up their apartment. He felt totally inadequate to carry out a superhuman task. Indeed he could *not* make the things happen that would cure his mom, restore her health, and reunite their family.

In the beginning of their difficulties, Tim's parents often argued. And Tim's sharp ears heard those fights that had to do with his childish pranks and necessary discipline. When his mother drank, he felt it was due to her frustration with him. And it was, he believed, largely his fault that his parents separated.

My time was nearly up, and I knew many reasons for Tim's problems in school. He was riddled with anxiety, consumed by his sense of guilt over his inability to work a miracle. But worst of all, in a voice brittle with the pent-up anger and fear of all his "tender" years, he unexpectedly blurted out, "I know how I'm gonna die!"

My next appointment was forced to wait as I gently teased out the story of Tim's planned suicide. He and his older brother would go out on their motorcycle, get the speed extremely high, and then crash. In a strangely loving way, they believed their family would consider it an accident and would not hurt as much as if they knew it to be suicide.

Many researchers believe many accidents of children and adolescents to be suicidal, and Tim's story certainly bears that out. Fortunately, in his case, his father was able to get the help Tim so desperately needed before that plan was carried out. But many children are not so fortunate.

Parents, please be alert to the possibility of allowing false guilt to pile up inside your child. When you are going through difficulties, it is easy to overlook the silent, hidden pain of a child who hears more than you would imagine. Without your wise explanations, he will guess at his own interpretations, and usually, these are inaccurate.

How to Heal a Guilt-Ridden Child

To prevent or heal the depression related to guilt, take these steps:

1. *Be aware.* A child covers and disguises his tender emotions. You must learn how to recognize them. Watch his face when he is not aware you are studying him. Remember, he is concerned about you, fearful of losing one or both of you, so he will try to find out what may be causing dissension.

2. *When there is a problem, discuss it openly.* Don't use your child as a confidante, and don't give her so many details that she will

worry. But do say, "Your mother and I are working on the family budget, and we don't always agree. So when we argue and even yell, don't worry. We're just trying to make our points. We will work it out, and we'll tell you about it." Or "You know, Son, Dad and I disagree about the way you ride your bike. He thinks you should go most anywhere you like because he did at your age. But I know our neighborhood has more traffic than his, so I worry about you. I want you to know that none of this is your fault, though. Dad and I will work it out soon so we can let you know where to ride." Clarification reassures your child and prevents self-incrimination.

3. *In disciplining your child, be cautious.* It is tempting to say, "You never make your bed. You're just a slob!" Such labels and generalizations are self-defeating. They make a child feel both guilty and helpless. If I am, in fact, a "slob," I'm very bad, and "never" is a long time. Try instead to say, "Last Tuesday you made your bed so neatly I know you can do it. And I love to walk into your room when it looks nice and reminds me of the really neat boy you are."

   In discipline, make the expectation clear, the time and method possible, and the consequences meaningful. Avoid using guilt as a "whip."

4. *Help your child recognize when he is truly guilty.* This is real guilt, not imagined as in Tim's case. When your child has done wrong or broken a rule, he must admit guilt and make it right as far as possible. Then the guilt needs to be forgiven and released.

   Helping children of elementary school age is relatively easy. They are usually willing to accept correction when it is given lovingly and balanced with earned praise. If your child shows signs of depression, either frank or disguised, seek help at once.

   Postponing the corrective measures that can readily relieve depression and restore optimism and success can make help ever so much more difficult. Step back and take a look at yourself. Make the necessary corrections, and then enjoy your child.

Depression in Young Children

1. *They are noticeably sad.* Much less likely to cover their hurts with anger than younger children, they will look sad. They will usually cry openly until they reach the "macho" age of ten (give or take a year).

2. *Within limits they will discuss their depression.* Depending on the strength of their relationships, they will talk with parents, teachers, neighbors, or other relatives about what they feel and even why. As they grow older, they are more likely to talk with their friends and may withdraw from adults.

3. *They refuse to discuss the problems very much.* Wendy wanted to solve her problem by her own method. To continue discussing it might have turned off further communication. Dropping comments and offering other possibilities usually work better than trying to force answers.

4. *Their academic work suffers.* When children are preoccupied with the anger and sadness that are parts of depression, how can they concentrate on reading or math? They often lack the mental energy to learn.

5. *They become moody.* They withdraw from usual activities. They spend time in their rooms just staring or escape through long TV-viewing sessions. They may snap at parents or act sullen. Moodiness is more pronounced in adolescence, but it is not unusual in younger children.

6. *Their social lives suffer.* Wendy refused to play with her friends for fear she would be hurt again. Tim, depressed over his mother's drinking habit, felt older and more burdened than his peers. Many depressed children simply haven't the energy to socialize.

7. *They may change physical habits.* Youngsters may seek solace through eating or sleeping too much or too little. To my knowledge, we have no scientific answers regarding why some overeat and others refuse food, but perhaps family patterns teach different responses.

8. *They may have suicidal thoughts or make a suicide attempt.* Children as young as six or seven may say, "I wish I was dead," or "Why do I have to live?" Few preadolescent children commit suicide, but the possibility is very real. Watch for extended periods of moodiness, the other seven signs, and hints children just "happen" to drop.

4

*Adolescents
and
Older Teens*

In only two decades, suicides of young people between ages fifteen and twenty-four have increased by 250 percent.[1] Each year I
must try to deal with the repercussions of the suicides of some ten
to twelve teenagers. Each death has an impact on other youths who
may see the death of a friend as a taunting temptation to escape
their own despair. Every person in the mental health field will repli-
cate my experiences again and again.

In a very careful piece of research, Robert Kosky and others
studied over six hundred children who were depressed and/or suicidal.[2] They discovered that children who thought seriously of suicide were more likely to have disturbed relationships with their
fathers and siblings than those who were simply depressed but not
suicidal. But both depressed and suicidal young people had disturbed relationships with their mothers. The disturbance was char-

1. James P. Comer, M.D., "Young Suicides," *Parents,* August 1982, p. 88.
2. Robert Kosky, et al., *The Journal of Nervous and Mental Disease,* vol.
174, no. 9, March 18, 1986, pp. 523–528.

acterized by persistent discord, persecution, hostility, and some form of child abuse.

So Parents, look carefully at the relationships within your families. I have learned that few parents *ever* want to hurt their children; they do so out of unconscious frustrations, severe stress, and inadequate resources for help. Later in this book I will offer a variety of resources for you.

Depression in Adolescents

His face, lined in sternness beyond his thirteen years, was downcast. It was embarrassing for Curt to show his tear-filled brown eyes to me—an unknown adult. But I could count the accelerating teardrops on his worn blue jeans. His sandy hair, though long and unruly, was clean. His nervous motion revealed the restless energy that drove him.

Another bright, capable student was failing most of his courses. And I, with my trusty magic wand, should make him better. But Curt had another, more serious, problem. He had confided in a friend that he was feeling "pretty down" and that he often felt like he'd rather not be alive. He spoke at other times of running away.

In getting to know Curt and his parents, I learned that they had discovered in kindergarten that he was unusually intelligent. He was also charming, good-looking, and fairly well accepted by his peers. Therefore, his parents had high expectations. They wished for him a higher level of success in life than they had achieved. So they were not content with *B*'s and *A*'s. They expected straight *A*'s. And despite Curt's ability, he did not give evidence in his intelligence tests of his ability to make straight *A*'s.

Feeling that his very best efforts were not good enough for Mom and Dad, Curt finally gave up. He decided to quit trying. He withdrew into his own sullen world of anger and sadness. He felt helpless and finally began to believe there was no hope. Curt was approaching despair—a situation that concerned me greatly.

Before I could reach his frustrated parents, Curt did indeed reach desperation. He swallowed a number of aspirin tablets, hoping to find release from an unbearable life in suicide. Fortunately, he did not take enough to do serious damage, but he certainly got the attention of his family!

Because they truly wanted the best for him, Curt's parents could not see their role in his problems. They believed that the school was too easy on him, that I was promoting "permissive parenting," that relatives were taking sides and just feeling sorry for him. And there was a little truth in what they said. But they could not accept that their input—of unwittingly expecting the impossible—had been a negative influence on Curt.

In almost all depression there are a series of losses—often forgotten and rarely gigantic. But because they have been unrecognized or forgotten, the grief work surrounding them has rarely been completed. It gradually collects until its weight breaks down the youth's defenses, leaving him sad, helpless, angry and, often, guilt-ridden.

Curt is a good example of a collection of such losses:

- He lost his carefree status as a child when he entered junior high and those "terrible teens."

- He lost his usual successes in elementary school to face stiffer competition and less help from teachers.

- He lost a trusting, secure relationship with one primary teacher to face a series of teachers who had large groups of students for less than one hour a day. He could find no way to know any of them well enough to feel understood or safe with them.

- Due to his depression and sullen withdrawing, he lost most of his friends. He didn't have the energy to care, really. He was too "down."

- Curt lost his parents' pride in him. The competency he had shown in elementary school was not evident to them after junior high. They believed he was just lazy, and they nagged, prodded, and punished instead of recognizing his need for comfort, reassurance, and encouragement. Curt needed to have study time established and responsibility enforced—but in a loving, supportive, and firm manner.

- Perhaps most painful of all was Curt's loss of confidence in himself. He came to believe that he could never make the leap to adolescence and that he would never again know success.

In addition to these losses, Curt's misery was compounded because he did not possess the physical stature, prowess, or coordination of many of his peers who cruelly teased anyone who was significantly different from themselves.

Depression in adolescence has several main causes, although its expression is similar for all of them. The expression, by the way, differs mainly according to each adolescent's temperament and the response of the adults involved with the individual.

1. A universal factor in depression is that of *some kind of loss*.

2. Almost as common in adolescents is a sense of being a *social misfit*. Feeling isolated or different from classmates is excruciatingly painful to a young teen who developmentally needs to identify with or belong to a group.

3. Being *physically different* from others is another focus of teen depression. The tall girl or the noticeably short boy (especially when he still has a boy-soprano voice) is going to attract attention.

4. Being *unable to compete* with some degree of success in sports is another cause of depression. In a culture that is almost as sports focused as it is sexually preoccupied, young people often seek peer acceptance and recognition through prowess in physical contests.

5. Depending on several factors, some young people who feel they *can never measure up* in other areas of life may try to compen-

sate through academic success. If this, too, fails to be possible, even more severe depression may set in.

6. Experiencing a *lack of parental encouragement and support* may serve as a distorted mirror to reflect the young adolescent's existing sense of ugliness. An affirming attitude from the family is always important, but to the adolescent, it is absolutely necessary.

Depression Look-Alikes

Although depression is extremely common in junior-high young people, they may behave at times as if they are depressed, but they actually are not. If you are to recognize and understand true depression, you need to know some of the attitudes and actions that resemble it. The following are five major look-alikes of depression.

1. *Fatigue Due to Rapid Physical Development*

As their bodies develop into adult, sexual ones, a great deal of physical energy is burned up. This process makes nearly all early adolescents somewhat lethargic at times.

Parents who fail to understand the physical aspects of adolescence may become impatient or worried. Sensitive, alert adolescents, even though they may *appear* lackadaisical, will quickly sense their parents' concern and will certainly react to parents' irritation. Any negative reaction by parents during these difficult months, and even several years, will complicate matters, often by precipitating needless depression.

I do *not* mean to imply that parents should "walk on eggs" or pamper adolescents. Nor should they give in to them in order to keep peace. Young teens desperately need parents who are wise enough to know when to extend limits and when to be firm enough to hold those lines tight.

Another priceless asset of parents is the ability to set limits and hold firm without *unnecessary* anger. Also avoid treating a teen in a childish manner. You need to rearrange your priorities very care-fully as your child is approaching puberty in order to have time to zero in on her needs and respond to them.

Before reacting to your child, consider these things:

- Is my son truly rude or rebellious, or is he trying to cover up the confusion and fear that belong to the no-man's-land between child and adult?

- Is my daughter defying me or testing me to see if I'm strong enough, wise enough, and caring enough to stand firm when I must?

- Am I reacting to my son in fear, holding him so tightly he'll have to rebel to get free of me at all?

- Do I ever correct my child by shaming her, even if I *intend* that to motivate her to try harder?

- Do I see my child as being lazy, pouty, or moody instead of truly fatigued and anxious about strange new thoughts and emotions?

- Have I complimented my child today?

- What am I doing today to prepare my child for successful adult-hood?

If you answer as few as three of these questions in a manner that is unsupportive of your child, I urge you to think before you react the next time. Your motives are almost certain to be positive, but your attitude may defeat the very help you intend to provide. If you cannot find an affirming, positive, loving frame of mind, seek help.

2. Disturbed Family Relationships

A friend brought his adolescent daughter to me for help. His shoulders inside his professional navy blazer were set in a firm line. His clean-shaven face depicted anger and resentments that nearly covered the anxious, tender look in his eyes. I occasionally detected the moisture of restrained tears as he related the struggles he and Melissa had endured. She was now depressed, he revealed, and at least 90 percent of the time a problem!

Believe me, I was eager to see a young teenager who was so extremely "bad." To my amazement, Melissa did not spit at me, swear at me, or act anything like a profoundly angry, depressed young woman. She was, in fact, very quiet and soft-spoken. Her long brown hair did cover her blue eyes, and she had a great deal of difficulty looking at me.

Over some weeks, Melissa and I became well acquainted. The problems her father had described were real, and they troubled her at least as much as they did him. She was perceptive enough to understand, as he had not, that the two of them were very alike. Such similar parent-child personalities often clash and result in severe misunderstandings.

When adolescents cannot resolve such difficulties through discussions, soften their parents with tears, or in any way known to them find harmony at home, they do one of three things: (1) withdraw to their rooms in moodiness, (2) spend more and more time away from home, or (3) resort to angry retorts. Melissa did all of these!

No wonder her father believed her to be depressed and just downright *bad!* But Melissa was not feeling helpless or guilty because she understood the situation fairly well. She knew she was no more at fault than her father. By her actions, she was proving she was *not* helpless (though she *was* at times misguided). She was frustrated at what she diagnosed as her dad's stubbornness. She was a bit sad because she really loved and admired her father but could not break through their barriers.

One of the joys of my profession as a therapist is that of helping restore harmony in dissonant families. As I sat one day with Melissa's father, I eagerly recounted Melissa's many assets, and I commented that he had raised a bright, loving daughter.

He looked incredulous. Surely she had "conned" me. She was still away from home or on the phone a lot; they could not communicate. Realizing I was not convincing him, I asked if he still believed Melissa to be 90 percent bad. Miserably enough, he nodded yes.

With a prayer for guidance I then suggested, "Bob, will you try for three weeks to ignore that 90 percent and react lovingly to the beautiful 10 percent?" After some thought, he agreed to try that as best he could.

I continued to see Melissa, encouraging her to react appreciatively to his efforts. A gradual change began to crescendo into a truly harmonious melody in that home.

These events took place some twenty years ago. Only a few months ago, I again saw my friend. With a grin, he thanked me for restoring his daughter to him. He had found that the more positively he reacted to her, the more open, loving, and appropriate she became. He couldn't quite give her 100, but he did say that she became 90 percent good. And I believe that's very good!

Parents may see their children as depressed when actually the young people are feeling shut out by their parents' unrealistic expectations. Believe it or not, teens want parental love and approval most of all when they act their very worst. And as I understand it, that's what the heavenly Father gave us—acceptance and forgiveness at our very worst.

3. Temporary Moodiness—The Blues

Cindy, eyes intently focused on her mirror, was a reflection of misery. Quietly, her mother watched for a while, then commented, "You look terribly unhappy, dear! What's bothering you?" She put down the clean laundry and sat expectantly on her daughter's rumpled bed.

It was a long wait, but worth every minute when Cindy finally broke away from her self-inspection. Wavy strawberry blonde hair in disarray, freckled cheeks wet with tears, and shoulders heaving with sobs, she threw herself into her mom's arms. At fourteen, that was, in itself, something of a task! Hugging her tall, gangly adolescent daughter was a not-so-common event, and both mother and daughter treasured the moments when they could recapture earlier times.

After her sobs quieted enough to permit words, Cindy began to explain. "Mother, why do I have to have curly hair and freckles? *No* one has such terrible hair. (The style was for long, silken, *straight* hair.) And not one of my friends has freckles. I'm fat and flat in all the wrong places. No boy will ever want to be seen with me. And I'm just *so* miserable!" The tears flowed again.

Mother rocked Cindy in an awkward teenage replica of her pre-school nap-time manner. She reminded her child that she, too, had freckles but that had only endeared her to Cindy's father when they were young. She offered hope that as Cindy continued to develop, the hated flatness would develop its curves, and with exercise and a careful diet she could help nature balance out a lovely figure.

Best of all, her mother pointed out, Cindy's own hurting was helping her to become kind and compassionate to others. It is, she said, not so much how one looks on the outside, but who one is becoming inside that counts. And it was clear to her mother that Cindy was pretty special—inside. Cindy was soon chatting away and smiling happily.

Certainly there were more grim tête-à-têtes with her mirror, more tears, more moods of both sadness and irritation, but Cindy would not be truly depressed. She was always sure of a wise confidante in her mother; she had enough friends, enough achievements, and enough common sense to remember the last time she felt "down" and her recovery.

All young teens have moments and sometimes hours of the "blues." Their own self-comparisons seem to leave them hopelessly beneath their peers. And because teens share their successes more easily than their sadness or fears, they may never realize that most of their classmates feel *exactly* the same way.

Fortunate, indeed, is the youth who, like Cindy, can turn to an understanding and available parent for comfort and counsel. Moments of pessimism can be transformed into realistic self-confidence and genuine compassion for others who have pain of some sort throughout life.

Adolescents suffer, often dramatically, over failing a test, being cut from the team, finding only a minor (or no!) part in a school play, being snubbed by the tragically snobbish cliques of their school. These and many other events create temporary disappointments and even moods of despair. But these are transient, lasting from a few hours to a few days, and they are interwoven with happy phone calls and plans for next weekend or next year.

The truly depressed person stays unhappy or even miserable for many days. Two to three weeks of constant hopelessness are usually necessary for a diagnosis of major depression.

4. Minigrief Episodes

One of the most common look-alikes of depression is grief. In fact, I must repeat that unresolved grief episodes accumulate and form the basis for most depression.

Whether it is a move away from a familiar existence, the loss of a grandparent, the divorce of a best friend's parents, or simply the lack of straight hair and clear skin, grief is the result—the common denominator of them all.

You parents need to recognize grief and distinguish it from depression. The main difference lies in the ease with which you can track down the grief's origin. You need to understand the concept of minilosses and the little grief that attends them. For these experiences, comfort and reassurance are all that are usually needed— along with time—to heal them.

In true depression, the victim can rarely recall any events that caused the sad feelings. And parents or school faculty members can rarely offer additional clarity. Professional counseling may be needed to unearth the beginnings of a lengthy, true depressive episode.

5. Chemical Addiction

Most serious drug and alcohol abuse, in my experience, is the result of underlying depression in young people. Even elementary-school children are enticed into the use of chemicals partly because they are bored or "blue." And with all the stresses of the turbulent early teens, it becomes almost irresistibly tempting to feel good quickly—with the help of a pill, a smoke, or a drink.

Many other youngsters, however, experiment with drugs or alcohol to be "in" with their so-called friends. They often become dependent on these chemicals and realize, too late, that they are caught in a web of stealing, engaging in sex-for-pay, and drug dealing to support a habit they feel they cannot break. This vicious cycle will almost surely end in depression, but there is grief, too—over the loss of freedom, individuality, and integrity. And these are tragic losses.

Parents, you must familiarize yourselves with the signs of chemical abuse: red eyes; dilated or pinpoint pupils in the eyes; a watery, itchy nose; the burnt-hemp odor of marijuana; lethargy and excitement occurring in cycles dependent on drug availability; long sleeves worn to cover needle marks; the unmistakable odor of various forms of alcohol. The school or your physician can supply you with literature on the subject. Obtain it and memorize it. Don't accuse your teen without good evidence, but never be lulled into the belief that such a tragedy cannot happen to your child.

Review of Signs of Depression in Adolescents

Let me summarize the major symptoms of serious depression in young adolescents.

1. *Their work suffers*. Adolescents' work is primarily academic, and usually the grades of depressed young persons suffer. Depression impairs the ability to concentrate, memorize, organize thoughts, and speak clearly.

   If they have job responsibilities around home, they have real difficulty getting even routine work done because of their preoccupation with their emotional pain and the energy drain it creates.

2. *Their social lives are damaged*. No one enjoys being around depressed persons, so friends often drift away. Furthermore, depressed young people stop reaching out to others. Even phone calls, the main joy in life to many adolescents, are cut off.

   Many depressed young people retain confidants, but they place those trusted friends in a serious bind. They swear them to secrecy, even about suicidal plans, but those friends are not equipped to carry such a heavy responsibility alone. Young persons who seriously consider suicide may give away special possessions or write notes about the disposition of prized items.

3. *Their emotions are different.* A young person who has been relatively quiet may become silly or clownish as a cover for depression. A youth who has always been effervescent may become irritable or silent. And these changes persist for weeks, in contrast to common moodiness of a few hours.

4. *Their physical habits change.* Eating habits seem to go to an opposite extreme from the "norm." Many depressed youngsters eat frequently and gain weight, but others refuse to eat and lose weight rapidly. The same holds true for sleep habits. Some sleep excessively, but others have great difficulty falling asleep, awaken with terrifying nightmares, or awaken early in the morning.

   The facial expression is a variable mix of anger, sadness, and anxiety. The shoulders usually slump, and the resting posture is strongly suggestive of depression. The weight of the world seems to rest on the young shoulders.

What to Do If an Adolescent Is Depressed

In this era of drug abuse, suicide, and all sorts of aberrant behaviors in youth, the very word *depression* strikes terror in the hearts of many parents. In fact, concerned parents often overreact and misinterpret normal adolescent development and behaviors.

1. I urge you, Parents, to *observe carefully,* wait watchfully, and seek input from others who are close to you and your children before you give in to anxiety. The symptoms listed are reliable, but your interpretation of them may be a bit out of proportion. Counsel from trusted friends, school counselors, a pastor, or your family doctor can verify your fears or reassure you.

   Remember the rule of thumb regarding the duration of the symptoms as well as their meaning. Your plump adolescent daughter may simply be slow in maturing to the level that she can control her eating habits. The door-slamming withdrawal of your angry son may simply be the only method he knows to avoid hitting his "crummy" kid sister.

If you are uncertain about your child's possible depression, ask what's bothering him. Don't blurt out a question in the midst of an angry confrontation. But perhaps at bedtime you can make a gentle comment: "Bill, I've been noticing that you are quieter than usual and you look sad. Can you tell me what's going on? I remember when I was just fourteen, life could seem awfully grim. If you can talk with me, I daresay I can help."

You may have to wait a long time for a truly depressed or even a moody child to talk. But that wait is well worth your time because it can release the pent-up pressure and cut short the mood. It may even be a positive turning point up and out of depression.

2. If the adolescent has at least four signs of serious depression that have lasted for as long as two weeks, by all means *consult with a counselor*. (See list at end of this chapter.) Locate one who truly knows family counseling and can help all of you to understand and overcome the problems together. It is widely recognized that the person in a family who seems to have "the problem" may be, like the tip of an iceberg, the smallest part of that problem. It always pays to check it out together.

3. *Use medications appropriately*. Many therapists these days depend on medications alone to relieve depression of patients. And believe me, medications can play an important part in treatment. They can be lifesaving if a person is considering suicide.

Many medications will relieve the signs of anxiety, worry, and depression. I frequently prescribe medications, but I believe that I have only begun my job when I write a prescription. My most vital task is to discover what caused the anger, sadness, guilt, fear, or helplessness that underlies the depression.

The old losses need to be understood, and the grief must be completed. The misunderstandings that create rifts between parents and child must be clarified; usually forgiving must take place. New insights must be acquired, and new choices need to be taught. Most people do not realize they have the power to choose how they will act or react or even how they will feel. Parents often fail to understand that their intended discipline may have been ill-fitting for a special child, resulting in estrangement and rebellion.

If you find a counselor who *only* medicates, please ask for or seek a second opinion. You and your child deserve the kind of help that will teach you how to recognize and cope successfully with stress without *forever* relying on a pill to do so for you.

4. In the process of counseling, I caution you to *avoid two common extremes*. At one extreme are families who stop too soon. It can feel so good to see some problems being solved that they may believe they have reached the end of the road to recovery. It usually takes some months to achieve the awarenesses family members need to prevent relapses.

At the other extreme are families who become so attached to the therapeutic process (or the therapist) that they become almost helplessly dependent. One primary goal in counseling is that of developing a trusting relationship with a person who cares about you and can help you. Equally important, sometimes painfully so, is the goal of personal growth in wisdom and loving strength that will result in independence from that therapist.

5. *Seek* as a counselor someone who will *help in your spiritual development* as well as in your understanding and communications. If you cannot find such a counselor, I urge you to meet regularly with a member of the clergy of your faith to keep your total life in balance. For a long time good counselors have been taught to avoid getting into the field of religion or faith. Fortunately, many therapists are learning that we are all spiritual beings as well as emotional, physical, and psychological ones. Many members of the clergy are also becoming aware of the need for good counsel along with spiritual growth. Keep your family well balanced by getting the help you need.

Depression in Older Teens

Each year news stories report the tragedies of young lives wasted through suicide. In 1984, over five thousand young people (ages fifteen to twenty-four) took their lives, according to the studies of the American Association of Suicidology in Denver, Colorado. At least three times that number consider suicide, according to a study done at the University of Kansas at Lawrence, Kansas, in 1986.

Personally, I have interviewed a great many seriously depressed, potentially suicidal young people. The causes of their depression are many, but some broad categories of causes may help us understand these youngsters who have lost hope.

Physical Changes

Puberty begins in junior high or sometimes even in elementary school. No specific time for its beginning and ending holds true for all people. The biological stress of physical development causes great changes in young people that can affect their lives.

When one person's change does not compare favorably with another's, that young person is at some risk for depression. A girl who is not as well developed as most of her peers is almost certain to suffer some degree of depression. The same thing is true of a young man whose pubertal changes lag far behind those of his friends. Skin problems, emerging sexual feelings, and ultimate body height and shape are physical issues that may contribute to late adolescent depression.

Social Factors

Being part of a group is a high priority among young people. Some established groups could become a place to belong, but due to social influences, many of them are not open to every young person. Only a select few can make it into a variety of athletic teams. A few more may belong to debate, drama, or music groups, and a very few become cheerleaders. Where do the vast number of teens belong? In many communities, there simply is no place for them.

True enough, many older teens find a niche in part-time jobs. The associates they find at work become friends and offer a social outlet. The money they earn provides some evidence of self-worth and offers the fun of spending the fruits of their own labors.

A tragically large group of young people find their place of belonging in groups of vandals, drug addicts, or alcoholics. The false highs and sophisticated pleasures these groups offer are tempting to youths who know too little success and have no self-esteem.

Our society has an extremely permissive attitude about sexual mores. Many youths in all sorts of groups become sexually active and even promiscuous at an early age. For many young people, sexual encounters are characterized by an intense, almost desperate quality. They think if they are considered "sexy," they will become popular.

Certain modes of dress and styles of hair have become symbols of the group to which teens belong. No single "look" prevails today. No longer is there a generalized appearance of shabbiness that characterized the teens of the sixties, and the designer labels of the late seventies and early eighties that robbed families' budgets are less conspicuous. Now we have the smartly dressed, affluent group, the counter-culture groups in army garb or "ethnic" wear, and the youths with extreme hairstyles and rock-group attire.

Each group has its levels—those who are leaders with some success and confidence, those who are followers and have some security in simply belonging, and those who simply don't fit, who feel strange, confused, and depressed. When these people find it impossible to locate a place for comfortable belonging, they are likely to consider suicide as the only escape from loneliness and futility.

Family Conflicts

As I've noted earlier, several studies show that troubled parent-child relationships contribute to depression throughout life. The disturbances may be of several kinds—neglectful, abusive, or over-protective. They often include divorce of the parents, alcoholism, or mistaken forms of discipline that weave the ugly strands of false guilt into the fabric of a child's personality.

Children who suffer pain from parents' mistakes are helpless in their misery. They learn to feel angry because it gives them a sense of some power. One adolescent confided that she had survived the almost unbearable pain of her earlier years by imagining taking her life. Considering life to be otherwise beyond her control, she found a measure of confidence in the capacity to decide to end it all if she needed badly enough to escape.

Other young people become depressed and contemplate suicide out of anger. Strangely enough, these youths actually know their parents care about them. They typically say, "I'll just kill myself! Then you'll be sorry!" Most young people who threaten suicide, and even those who attempt it, do not actually want to die. They are screaming out the anguish of their frustration at life—and often specifically at their families.

They very often take a handful of whatever prescription drug they find in the medicine cabinet or just common pain relievers. Some of them carve lines across their wrists or over a vein elsewhere, and many cut designs of some sort on their bodies. Thankfully, most instances of self-mutilation and pill swallowing are only gestures, dramatic cries for help or attempts to escape imagined or real threats of punishment.

But such actions should *never* be dismissed lightly. Whether or not their lives are at stake, they are asking in the best way they know for help. And they may accidentally take too many pills, cut a bit too deeply, or miss out on the anticipated "rescue" if help does not arrive. Life is a precious gift to be saved and restored to joy!

Academic Stress

Pressures to achieve academic success are strong in a great many families and schools. In fact, there is an upsurge in visits to therapists during times when grades will be released. Only a few years ago, a friend's youngest son disappeared from home one evening in late spring. My friend and her husband adored their son, and they tried to provide the proper balance in tough and tender love that would make him a secure, well-balanced person.

They were incredulous, then, to hear from his friends that he had run away from home shortly before he was to graduate from high school. During the hours he was gone, they suffered immeasurable anxiety. Desperately, they reviewed their imagined or real mistakes in an attempt to understand why he would leave home.

After what seemed like an endless day to the parents, their wandering son returned. His story was simple. During the last quarter of his senior year, he had become careless about studies. Frankly, he didn't know what he wanted to do with his life, and he was somewhat anxious and depressed. When his grades came out, he was appalled at their decline. He simply panicked, imagined his parents would be devastated, and could not face their disappointment in him. They were upset about the poor grades, but they were able to reassure their son that they would always love and help him through anything.

When teens are unable to succeed academically, they are likely to become depressed. The more depressed they are, the less effectively they can study, and their grades fall even more. When parents yell and punish truly depressed young people, they further complicate those problems and estrange their children.

Our schools, to complicate matters further, do not help the problem. Over the years, they have rigidly attempted to press all young people into one academic mold. Certainly all people need basic skills in reading, mathematics, and communications. All students, however, are not college-bound, nor should they be. Many trades demanding a variety of skills are just as essential as academic excellence. Mechanical work of all sorts is fundamental to the maintenance of our civilization, but schools fail to emphasize this. The trades are still relegated to positions of less respect in some families and reserved for those who can't go on to college.

If your teenager can't concentrate on English or has difficulty with math, help him to learn these basics the best he can, and then introduce him to a variety of career opportunities, such as carpentry, plumbing, tailoring, or food service, among others. Let your teen discover the future for which his inborn talents and natural interests fit him. You can help him avoid depression by finding fulfillment and a focus for his skills.

Drugs

The hard young face opposite me was almost frightening. Dick was only sixteen, and he was already an angry failure. His high IQ was denied by the list of *F*'s on his grade report. His eyelids drooped, and his speech was not always audible. When I finally aroused him enough to talk, he verified my guess. He had been smoking "pot" with friends before school that very morning.

His gang came to school early and gathered, of all places, under the stairs of a nearby church. They took turns providing marijuana and believed they were putting one over on both their parents and the school staff. This boy had no idea that the drug was slowly taking control of him. It was making him lose motivation, hampering his ability to concentrate and remember, and giving him a false sense of power.

Marijuana, speed, cocaine, and all illegal drugs are deceptive, and they breed a vicious cycle. Many young people start taking drugs out of curiosity or to get an easy "high." Before they realize it, they become drug dependent, and then they become frightened and depressed.

Other teens start on drugs because they are unbearably depressed, and the chemicals help them feel better—for a while. But then they become even more depressed because they run out of money to buy the substance and are afraid their parents will find out. Their suppliers promise help if they will sell for them, and a complex fear-and-need-based system is established.

Parents and school faculty must join resources to recognize the depression that makes students vulnerable to drug dealers and dealing. Courses should be developed about drugs and about depression. And counseling and support should be required before such tragic addiction destroys our young people and our culture. All too often, parents believe depression is just a phase and fail to seek help. They may punish their child's behavior and fail to understand and support his sagging self-esteem. Many schools now offer excellent help for both depressed teens and their parents. This should be used.

Broken Relationships

In the late teens and early twenties most young people form relationships of permanence. (At least we used to consider them permanent!) Dating develops much more seriously, and the possibility of engagement and marriage becomes a probability at this stage.

When everything goes smoothly and progress is made toward a commitment, all is well. But that is not always what happens. In some instances sweethearts change their minds and break their promises and even engagements. A very secure young person will grieve over a rejection of this magnitude, recover, and find a new partner.

However, the broken dreams and sense of rejection that this event involves may throw a person into deep depression. Anyone who has suffered previous fractures in a serious relationship and who has poor self-esteem is a likely candidate for this sort of emotional breakdown.

The devastating part of rejection is the implication that the one who is left is not really a very good person. The one the sweetheart favors is obviously perceived as the better person. So it is not breaking up, alone, that is the problem. It is the unfavorable comparison the rejected person sets up that lands a powerful blow to the ego.

(*Note:* Up to this section of the book, I have addressed parents primarily. But I think that this subject and the one that follows it are more appropriately addressed to the young person.)

At this very point, you may find your greatest resource. Rather than give in to the supposition that the new person is superior, think carefully and evaluate honestly. It is almost certain that you are as capable and likable as the new love. You simply may not fit the personality and meet the needs of your erstwhile sweetheart as well as the new love. Chances are that neither you nor your prospective partner would have been very happy if the marriage had taken place. Another strong possibility is that your onetime sweetheart is fickle, has trouble with choices, and is habitually searching for greener pastures.

Once you establish your basic worth, you will be far better prepared to cope with depression. That does not mean, of course, that you should rationalize away all your faults. You may well have habits or attitudes that do not wear well in an intimate relationship. Use this pain to goad you into a bit of healthy introspection. Whatever you discover that is not as positive as you would like it to be can be changed. Ask a friend to remind you when you slip into habitual behaviors that offend others. You can become even more lovable by working on change and growth.

The Future

Rick loved to tinker with tools. Ever since he was a little boy, he had been fascinated with fixing broken things and building new items. A cherished memory was of his grandfather showing him how to use a chisel and saw.

In high school Rick realized he hated books, and he did not make good grades. For many young men, this would have been no serious problem, but for Rick, it seemed a giant issue. He greatly respected his father and wanted to please him. He knew all too well what his dad expected of him. Dad was an attorney and had, in his own opinion, become far more successful than Rick's mechanic grandpa. In fact, Rick believed his father held little respect for the old man who tinkered in his shop and earned little money.

The predicament is clear and is representative of what happens to many young people. Rick wanted to measure up to his dad's expectation that he enter a profession, but he realized he probably could not achieve the academic proficiency to do so. In his heart he wanted to follow his grandfather's trade, but he felt to do so would lose him his dad's respect. The dilemma was constantly on Rick's mind, and the depression generated by his helplessness became serious. To avoid his anxiety, Rick began to drink and, of course, to neglect his studies. Though he entered college, his depression and dilemma were packed with his other belongings into his suitcases.

Whether in high school, college, or the early stages of being out on your own, the challenge is there. When you grow up, who do you want to be? How can you find out? Who will help you? Are you willing to practice the self-discipline and even sacrifices it will take to reach your goals?

The world is changing rapidly. Many jobs that once were attached to manufacturing things in this country no longer exist since we import the items. Jobs now seem to focus on services, but these positions are scarce since so many people are seeking to make a living in service-related industries. Knowledge has exploded in recent decades. How can you master all you need to learn? These big questions may seem to have no answers, and depression is likely to overpower you.

Signs and Symptoms

Depression in Adolescents and Older Teens

1. *A subjective feeling of sadness and hopelessness.* They can seem to find no way out of their maze of stress and inadequacy. This inner feeling can be picked up by careful observers of their facial expression, posture, and tone of voice.

2. *Moodiness.* A clear demonstration of sadness and hopelessness, moodiness may well be masked by irritability or downright anger. Almost all youths have these feelings at some time, but truly depressed young persons will experience them for weeks at a time.

3. *A bleak outlook for the future.* Seriously depressed youths make no plans for next week or next year. I worry about suicide when young people express no hope for anticipated happiness at least after the crisis is over.

4. *Disturbances of eating*. They may eat too much or too little, but there is a prolonged change in eating patterns from their normal ones. Anorexia and bulimia have become common diagnoses and are extremely frequent. These cases involve several emotional and familial issues, but a distinct element of depression is usually involved.

5. *Sleep disturbances*. They may have frightening dreams. They may have difficulty in getting to sleep or awaken early due to the inner stress of the many anxieties and problems in which they feel immersed. Or they may sleep excessively.

6. *Changes in social life*. They are likely to stop spending time with friends. They may even refuse phone calls. Rarely, a usually withdrawn young person may enter almost feverishly into social activities to lift himself out of despair.

7. *Chemical abuse*. Some young people begin using drugs and alcohol out of curiosity or to prove their sophistication, but most of them do so to relieve depression. Before they know it, they are "hooked" and unable to stop.

8. *Suicidal ideas*. Preadolescents often leave notes or drawings around that clearly allude to depression and death. In my experience, this is infinitely more true of adolescents and older teens.

The answers to this sort of depression are truly difficult to find. But here are some ideas that can help.

1. Try to forget the ambitions and demands of everyone else for a while. Think carefully about your inner strivings. When you were seven or ten, what did you most enjoy doing? What did you want to be when you grew up? Inner searching may put you clearly in touch with your own best goals and aptitudes.

2. Ask your parents or, better yet, your grandparents what they think you are good at doing. Teachers or friends may also be helpful in this search.

3. Be practical. What education and training opportunities are open to you? Consider your intellectual skills, financial resources, and personal aptitudes. What jobs are likely to be available if and when you complete a specific training program?

4. If you can find no workable solutions, seek out a vocational counselor. In high schools and many junior colleges, services are available to evaluate your aptitudes. They pick up the areas you are likely to be good at and can tell you what kinds of jobs may be available and even what it will take to prepare you for such jobs.

5. Make a genuine commitment to stick with your training until you are prepared to excel in the field you choose.

6. Most career decisions can be changed. Do not get stuck in the process of choosing by the fear that you may dislike a certain field but then never be able to leave it. Many an initial career choice becomes only the gateway into something an individual would not otherwise have considered.

Even as you investigate some possibilities for your future, I hope you will discover your depression is dissipating. Depression cannot long coexist with decisive action and commitment to excellence. You can choose to become who you want to be as well as how you want to feel and act. Our Creator has given us this incredible power!

Please review the signs and symptoms of depression in this chapter. If you have four or more of these, focus on your life. You may be able to find out what factors are at work to create your disorder. If you know, make a plan to solve the problems. If you don't know, talk about your situation and your feelings with a perceptive friend or a counselor. Never accept the belief that seeking help means you are crazy or weak. The opposite is, in fact, true. It takes courage and honesty to face your needs, admit you need help, and follow through to solutions. The exciting truth is that you can find the answers to your special needs!

Accept the fact that your teenage years will be turbulent. The physical changes are drastic; social adjustments and relationships are changeable and may be disappointing; facing the future with its demands for adult responsibilities is frightening; becoming independent from parents is confusing and difficult.

Parents' need to release older adolescent children to become adults is equally frightening. They often instinctively grasp their children and try to rework their discipline and training, creating needless rebellion. A key to surviving these times is the parents' ability to remember (to recall their own youth), to recapture the good job they actually did (a day at a time) as parents, and to rely on the master plan God designed for them and their young adult child.

5

Young Adults and New Parents

While the turbulence of adolescence is trying and depression both common and severe, the young adult years carry their share of difficulties, as well. The excitement of dating and early marriage give way to the trials of adjusting to routine family life and balancing responsibilities with pleasure. A new baby or two create frightening demands that have no visible end.

For those who postpone marriage in favor of advanced schooling or job training, there is pressure to compete and succeed. The need to measure up to specifications laid down by others can become oppressive. Young adults, too, carry a high risk for depression and its occasional manifestation of suicide.

Depression in Young Adults

Perhaps the young adults at greatest risk are college students. They have so much to prove about themselves in such a highly competitive environment. Feeling lonely on a crowded campus can be the greatest rejection in the world. Seeing others finding successes greater than one's own, and with apparent ease, can be devastating to a student's ego.

The cost of college is great and instills, even in more ungrateful young persons, some sense of obligation. If they do not make the grades to justify the spending of all that money, an immeasurable sense of worthlessness and hopelessness may overwhelm them. If the parent-child relationships are less than secure, college students may become depressed and even suicidal.

A sign of severe depression and likely suicide is that of giving away treasured possessions. Sometimes they will write out a "will" giving away special items to family members and friends. Dropping comments implying that they have no hope or that they feel impending doom is another serious sign. *Feeling* blue or hopeless is one thing. *Believing* that there is no hope in this world is quite another.

Later on, we will discuss the depression of singles and the predicaments of those who must parent children alone. There are a number of situations that can create stress and depressions in young adults.

Many young adults are unable to find a person to marry. They may have grown up in families that were torn by constant disagreements or even divorce. It is widely believed that young women are unhappy in marriage, find their husbands disappointing, and life far from fulfilling. If this is true, both women and men will feel inadequate, as if they are failures, and are candidates for depression.

The inability to find and marry that "right" person becomes a problem not only to young people but to their parents who would like to enjoy grandchildren. The sense of being un-chosen must feel like a rejection. Many young people I know simply escape their loneliness and depression by frequenting bars. Through alcohol and transient, superficial relationships, they desperately try to find excitement.

The young couples who yearn for children are another category of depressed people. To go through every test, take every prescription, and try everything possible, and still be unable to have a baby can be extremely disappointing. Many infertile couples feel inadequate and may even believe that God is withholding parent-hood as some sort of punishment.

If success eludes young adults, they may become depressed. This is a competitive world, and those who climb to top positions with high salaries may *feel* good. If they suffer losses, however, they may lack the inner core of ego strength to cope. Such persons fall prey to severe depression. Those who do not reach the peaks of success they dreamed of may feel they have totally failed and also give in to depression.

Countless types of disappointments, struggles, or losses may afflict young adults. To whom should they turn? Returning to par-ents is possible, but it may represent total failure and giving up. To turn to friends may reveal weakness, and fear of being rejected pre-vents many from seeking support there. Some find help in psycho-therapy and a very few in religious resources. But many live lives of borderline failure, seeking relief in illegal drugs or such excitement as they can find.

But for all, there is hope. You can overcome depression and find joy and fulfillment in living.

Depression in New Mothers

Baby Becky stretched and wriggled as she awoke from her after-noon nap. Her empty tummy was uncomfortable, and even though she was just ten days old, she wanted to be near her mother. Becky fussed a bit, then she whimpered, and soon she was wailing loudly. Babies do not understand why parents are slow to respond to their needs and wishes.

Becky's mother, Marilyn, was tired. She still had pains from the baby's delivery, and her breasts were miserable. She felt imprisoned by the recurrent needs of the child to be fed, bathed, changed, and totally cared for. Marilyn's tummy was far from being the trim, flat one she had anticipated, and the excess weight she had believed would magically disappear at Becky's birth was still sticking to her body. No matter what angle she posed, her mirror said, "You're fat and ugly!"

That's how Marilyn felt, and despite all her efforts to overcome it, she believed that her misery was actually Becky's fault. She resented the child and all the work, inconvenience, and demands she created. At times Marilyn blamed her husband, Greg. He had wanted this child so much. If only he hadn't, she might not be saddled now with more work and responsibility than she ever dreamed existed. She could be dressing up and going to the job she loved and out to lunches with the other young women in the office.

Marilyn did not sleep well at night because she was afraid some dreadful thing might happen to Becky. She knew about SIDS (sudden infant death syndrome), and she had heard of a baby getting its head caught between the slats on the crib. In spite of her frustrations and misery, she loved Becky. What a perfect miniature person she was!

Marilyn faced a dilemma. She knew she and Greg were blessed to have a perfect baby like Becky. Yet she simply could not face the demands that were woven through every part of her existence. Marilyn felt trapped in her predicament, she was angry and sad, and she felt guilty about her feelings.

Certainly Marilyn was depressed, and her depression deepened rather than lessened as the days passed. She finally called her doctor.

Since most of her difficulties were connected to the birth of her baby, her doctor diagnosed her as suffering from *postpartum depression*. (The term *postpartum* means "after delivery.") He kindly explained some of her difficulties and reassured her that many new mothers go through such feelings. Some of her problems, he told her, were related to physical issues.

Carrying fifteen pounds of extra weight was no small burden in itself, especially when she had expected it to magically melt away. He gave her a good, adequate diet that allowed her to have plenty of milk for Becky, but she could lose a few pounds of fat at the same time.

The nurse taught her some exercises that were not too fatiguing but would help restore her appearance and improve her energy level. She encouraged Marilyn to go for a walk every day when

Greg could watch Becky. Symbolically, Marilyn came to understand that walking not only helped her regain physical fitness; it also represented the fact that she was not *totally* attached to her new baby. With proper planning, she could find increasing bits of time for herself. She need not, after all, be only a slave.

Because Marilyn wanted to nurse Becky, the doctor could not prescribe medication. Had she been much more depressed, however, he may very well have offered her a carefully selected medication to reestablish her normal feelings and functioning more quickly.

Finally, Marilyn's physician recommended an excellent counselor. He chose a woman who, he knew, would understand her feelings and yet would not sympathize too much. He knew that overly sympathetic counseling could make Marilyn feel even more sorry for herself.

In the process of her counseling, Marilyn learned a great deal that was to help her become a happier mother and a better person. She had grown up in a very loving but overprotective family. Her mother expected very little from Marilyn except to be happy and good. Generally, she was both.

There were few things Marilyn ever wanted that her doting father failed to secure for her. He was extremely fond of his only daughter, and he generally believed he could make everything okay for her.

She had grown up in a sheltered, secure, magical world. True, she had little power, but then she needed very little. She had fun, was pretty and charming, well-loved and successful enough in school to get by. She discovered, however, that her personality development had slowed to a near standstill in her adolescence. She had focused her life on fun with just enough work to pay the costs of pleasure. Marilyn had not learned to postpone present pleasure for future good, and she was not at all skilled in self-discipline.

In spite of her charm, Marilyn had to face the fact that she was a pampered child who had a lot of maturing to do. Her baby was the first force in her life powerful enough to put such a commitment into focus for her. She would have a great deal of work to do, but Marilyn knew Becky and her marriage were worth working for.

And she recognized that after a while, Greg would grow weary of her childishness that was as often selfish and difficult as it was "cute" and fun.

Marilyn also learned that a normal grief process accompanies the birth of a baby. The loss that sets in motion the grieving is often overlooked. It would seem that the birth of a baby is purely a wonderful gift—a new life, a combination of mother and father, a product of their love.

But the advent of every child is accompanied by a profound loss—the loss of carefreeness. Throughout life there is a pattern of an increasing loss of freedom—from toilet training and weaning, to kindergarten and first grade, through school, jobs and promotions, marriage, children, and even retirement. Gains are achieved mainly through loss, the loss of time, energy, and freedom for the self in the interests of other people, demands, and activities.

Every mother who experiences the "baby blues" does not need extensive psychotherapy. Recently, a beautiful young first-time mother called with the tearful voice and melancholy manner so typical of depression. We discussed for only a few minutes some of the facts of postpartum depression, and she spent a little more time talking it over with her husband. She has graciously permitted me to include her follow-up letter.

> *I thought I'd jot you a note to let you know I'm doing great! Things seemed to clear up as quickly as it all came on. In looking back over last week, I observed several things. First, I wonder if part of my depression was physical because throughout my bad days I had repeated "hot flushes" where my face would "burn." I had those same sensations after Timothy was born—but only occasionally. Last week, however, I had them very often throughout the day. And now they have cleared up.*
>
> *Along with that were sweeping feelings of emotions where I felt like weeping. The strange part of this ordeal was that I had little control over my feelings. Without warning, these terrible despairing, depressing feelings came on. Sometimes during the day I'd feel better and more optimistic, and then the feelings would sweep over me again.*

Young Adults and New Parents

For some reason while I was feeling so depressed, I couldn't shake a terrifying dream about my baby and felt terrible for having dreamed such a horrible thing about him. The more I tried to shake it off—the more I thought about it and the worse I felt. So, as you can see I was really all worked up in no time at all.

I also realized after talking to you that there were things I was "grieving" over. I was grieving over my "battle-scarred" body with all its stretch marks and extra weight. I wondered if my husband would still be attracted physically to me. I shared those fears, by the way, with Jeff after talking to you, and the endearing words he spoke to me are ones I'll remember for a long time!

I also grieved over the loss of time for myself as well as the freedom to come and go. I thought I was ready for all the changes a baby brings, but when it came right down to it, I wasn't really prepared. Last week I couldn't enjoy Timothy at all—just went through the motions, and of course that made me feel like a rotten mother, which added to all the other feelings I was having. I spent much time praying and reading the Bible to keep my head above water, and Jeff was also a great support. Then on Monday, I woke up feeling fine! I wasn't plagued by the nightmarish thoughts, and I had a good day with Timothy. I've felt my normal self since.

Some good things have come out of last week, even though I never want to go through that again. For one, Jeff and I are closer because it opened up talking about our feelings. For another, I realized that although I love being a mother and enjoy Timothy so very much, I can't expect to have the kind of deep love I have for someone I've known much longer. I think bonding takes time. I also realized I was "hovering" over Timothy too much and needed to let Jeff do more with him as well as my getting away more. I decided to get back to my free-lance writing I had abandoned when I got pregnant. So, I do believe God used a difficult time to show me some things.

I want to thank you, Grace, for talking with me. It felt better to know I was still normal—and not losing my mind. I think I let my fears get the best of me. Perhaps I can thank you by being available to other young moms going through a similar time just as you were available to me.

The Many Faces of Depression

When expectant mothers do not realize the impact of losing freedom and assuming responsibilities, they are extremely vulnerable to postpartum blues—and even real depression. And expectant fathers may have a similar experience.

New Fathers and the Blues

The slump of his shoulders told me at once that Matt was feeling "down." Sitting in the big wingback chair in my office, he almost folded into its soft upholstery. His voice sounded hollow and weak, and the tears, coursing down his cheeks, caused him great embarrassment. Matt was a new father of a very much wanted baby boy. He had been excited about Larry's anticipated birth and was in awe of the changes in his wife's body that helped form the creative miracle of this new life.

But now, Matt was all too aware, he was depressed. He had realized that for several weeks, he'd been resenting the inconvenience of having little time alone with Lana, his wife. The problems of finding a sitter made it hardly any fun to go out. They were used to doing fun things spontaneously—but no longer. Larry's demands on Lana seriously depleted her energy and robbed Matt and Lana of their special intimacy. And Matt felt awkward with Larry, even though he was nearly six months old.

Furthermore, Matt mourned, the costs of the baby's care were unbelievable. Without Lana's income they were barely balancing their budget. Larry had to have his regular medical checkups, and his immunization shots were expensive. Then he used more and more diapers, and he outgrew clothes with great regularity. The doctor wanted them to start Larry on baby foods, and they were expensive, too.

Besides all the problems Matt listed, he made it quite clear that worst of all was his emotional reaction to the issues. He felt so helpless! And being a man, of course, he should not be so weak. He mentally berated himself because he should, he believed, be proud and happy. He felt guilty about his resentments and anxieties. He felt resentful of Lana's neglect of him, but he was glad she was being a good mother. Matt, like Marilyn, was experiencing the postpartum blues.

It was easy to help Matt understand the facts of his extreme losses—loss of freedom, loss of time for intimacy with his wife as well as her support of him and his job (he was used to that), loss of enough money for his personal interests and fun, and loss of his peace of mind. What a list to contemplate!

Matt was insightful enough to realize that losses always precede grief. He was hurting badly, but he did know the stages and process of grieving. He was already through with the first stage—denial. For several months, he realized, he had been trying to deny his negative feelings and overlook his losses. After all, he and Lana *should* be happy with their new boy. But his very presence in my office, along with his tears and outpouring of emotions, revealed that he could no longer deny reality.

Denial is the first stage of grief. Next follows anger, often accompanied by blame. The third stage is preoccupation with the loss and the emotional pain that goes with it. Very often there are touches of guilt and self-pity that complicate and prolong the process. Finally, there comes a resignation that accepts the loss and the helplessness to change or even reduce that loss. Almost miraculously, after the resignation, healing begins, and at some point, joy and peace return.

It was quite clear to both Matt and me that he was in the second stage of grief, anger. It was still difficult for him to focus that anger, but mainly it was the outcropping of his discovery that parenthood was *not* all it was portrayed to be. He felt deceived by life and cheated of the joys he had anticipated.

Matt really tried, however, to focus the anger on someone. If only his parents had taught him better! If only Lana would pay a *little* less attention to Larry, she could find time for him. If only they had waited another year to have a baby. Matt painfully talked his way through the blaming and finished the stage of anger.

He also faced the fact that he was indulging in a poor-me game. Frankly, at first he had enjoyed feeling sorry for himself, but that was getting tedious. He really wanted to feel good again. He cut short his "self-pity" detour of grief.

As he talked openly with other new dads, he was surprised to discover that they shared many of his feelings. Some of them were even considering leaving their wives because of jealousy over the attention given to the babies. Matt realized that having feelings is okay but that using them or acting them out destructively is wrong.

With these discoveries, Matt's guilt melted away since he had *done* nothing wrong. His fear of being abnormal disappeared when he learned most fathers feel similarly at times.

Next he worked on the third stage, his preoccupation with the painful helplessness and anxiety he was experiencing about providing for his family. He and Lana found they could save several dollars a week by using and laundering cloth diapers. By careful budgeting, they could make it, and Lana could do some office work for small neighborhood businesses in her home while Larry slept.

I encouraged Matt to find someone to care for Larry now and then to give Lana a break and restore some time for them to renew their marriage. Both of them discovered that this worked a miracle in their relationship. Lana had not realized that she was unnecessarily devoted exclusively to their wonderful new child, and she was as happy as Matt to have time together again.

When Matt finally accepted the fact that it would never be *convenient* to be a parent, he reexperienced peace of mind. His resignation (the next to last stage of grief) was, to his amazement, followed by joy. At last, Matt felt, he had become a real dad. And now he and Lana could find genuine fulfillment in each other and in their special gift, Larry. Healing was completed.

Without the information and understanding Matt had gained, I can safely predict, he would very likely have become severely depressed. He may even have left his family to try to meet his own needs in a selfish manner. So many young fathers do this rather than admit they have needs that require special help.

Anticipate the Changes

Since sharing Matt's grieving and celebrating with him his prompt recovery, I have been working with several young couples to prevent depression (as it often becomes).

Ginny and Sam were so excited about their pregnancy. They had waited for six years to begin their family, and Ginny was only two months away from her due date. When I asked them if they had begun to experience the anxiety and sadness of becoming new parents, they looked at me in surprise. Surely Dr. Grace had "lost it." Was she going just a bit crazy? I assured them I hadn't and wasn't, and I recommended they think about ways in which their home and relationship would be different after their baby actually arrived.

The next time I chatted with them, Sam hugged me with tears in his eyes. He had been able to imagine Ginny feeding, rocking, and playing with that new baby as he sat awkwardly nearby or escaped to his workshop to avoid feeling crowded out. By considering such events and feelings ahead of time, he had been able to short-circuit the denial and anger. He was still feeling some of the sadness on their way to the hospital. But by the time the new baby came home, Sam had almost finished grieving. He was able to allow Ginny time with the baby, but he also insisted that he take over sometimes, giving himself a chance to bond with his child, Ginny time for herself, and both of them time for each other.

Anticipating the grief and working through it ahead of time were new ideas to me, but I have seen new parents prevent depression and emotional separation at the birth of a baby when they have taken time to do these things.

Let's review seven important facts about postpartum depression:

1. It is due, in part, to hormonal and other physical changes in new mothers.

2. It is extremely common and not abnormal as a rule.

3. It can become a problem if it is ignored or denied. Then it can grow to be really serious.

4. It is largely due to misconceptions, the loss of freedom, and the changes in the total life-style of a couple.

5. It is shared in some degree by fathers as well as mothers.

6. It will recur with succeeding births, though usually with less intensity due to the awareness of having survived the previous time.

7. It can usually be prevented by facing the losses and working through the grief early on.

If you, like Marilyn, have been dumped precipitously in this sort of depression and can't work your way out, I urge you to seek professional counseling. This need not take long. Matt required only a few visits to work through his grief and early depression, preventing a more serious condition.

Marilyn's situation, superimposed on some personality weaknesses, took a bit longer. But even she became a far healthier person emotionally for having gone through the entire experience. Without counseling, however, I suspect she would have been left more vulnerable rather than more mature and strong.

I hope you are beginning to share with me my optimism regarding overcoming and preventing depression!

SIGNS AND SYMPTOMS

Depression in Young Adults and New Parents

1. *Loss of interest* or pleasure in all or almost all usual activities and pastimes. They feel blue, sad, hopeless, or irritable and may look sad.

2. *Changes in dietary patterns,* such as poor appetite and weight loss (without planned dieting) or increased appetite and weight gain.

3. *Sleep disturbances* characterized by lack of sleep or too much sleep.

4. *Changes in level of activity* resulting in hyperactivity (restlessness) or unaccustomed inactivity.

5. *Loss of interest in sexual activity.*

6. *Loss of energy* and a sense of fatigue.

7. *Feelings of worthlessness,* self-reproach, or guilt.

8. *Difficulty in thinking* and concentrating and trouble in making decisions.

9. *Recurrent thoughts of death,* wishes to be dead, and suicidal thoughts or attempts.

6

Middle-Aged Women

The older I become, the more difficult it is to define middle age! Life expectancy is now about seventy-five years, so middle age would begin at about thirty-five—give or take a little. This chapter refers primarily to women, but many principles could just as clearly apply to men.

There is a drop in severe depression after thirty-five years of age as measured by the decline in suicide rates. However, the members of this age group experience a great deal of anxiety, worry, and mild depression. As they try to compete in the work force, establish a marriage, and raise young children, mature adults are often too busy to take stock of their lives.

When they fail to succeed as highly as they dreamed, when income and material possessions are not as magnificent as those of their friends, when children have problems, and when marriage is not, after all, very satisfying, depression is likely to result and take its toll.

In adults, as in children, depression has its taproot in the past. Careful research by several people makes it clear that adult depression is associated with disturbed parent-child relations. These disturbances include too little parental nurturing, support, and affection and too much parental rejection.[1]

The signs and symptoms of depression in this age group are essentially the same as those for young adults and new parents. The exact symptoms will vary from person to person depending on temperament, personality, habits of behaving and feeling, and genetic and biochemical factors (that is, factors that have been inherited and are influenced by body chemistry).

By the age of forty-five to fifty, the occurrence of depression increases due to facing the inevitability of aging. In women we call this the menopause, something we face with mixed emotions. It is a relief to be free of those annoying cycles of discomfort and irritability associated with menstruation. On the other hand, as wrinkles increase and the sagging of our bodies cannot be controlled with the best of exercises, we realize that we will never be physically what we once were.

Nature prepares us women for our menopause and its inevitability from the time of puberty. Men, on the contrary, have a tougher time accepting the reality of the physical limitations of aging, and many of them experience what has come to be known as *the male midlife crisis*. Unfortunately, at this time some men choose to leave their wives of many years in favor of younger women. So, what was originally a problem for middle-aged men becomes a problem for middle-aged women.

We must add the grief and depression of abandoned older women to our list of middle-aged problems. Many of them heroically rise to their situation. They return to school, find jobs, and reestablish their social lives with dignity and strength—a great cure for depression!

1. Daniel J. Burbach and Charles M. Borduin, "Parent-Child Relations and the Etiology of Depression," *Clinical Psychology Review,* vol. 6, 1986, pp. 133–153.

Depression in Middle Age

Various researchers in both Europe and the United States show that some 18 to 23 percent of women and 8 to 11 percent of men at some time in adult life have a serious bout with depression. Many of them suffer severely enough to require time in a hospital for treatment.[2] Actually, if we were able to study the silently depressed people who cover up their symptoms, I suspect those percentages would be doubled or tripled.

Depression in midlife is complex and has many factors that combine to cause it.

1. *The body is aging.* All sorts of wear and tear on the body result in quite obvious signs of aging. Many women are entering into the menopause. Wrinkles, gray hairs, and sagging body tissues can no longer be ignored. Even the best of creams, hormones, and vitamins will not deter the effects of the relentless march of time. In a culture that values youth and beauty, the helplessness and grief women feel at losing these may be intense and may result in depression.

2. *Dreams remain unfulfilled.* Many of us have dreams about life that date back to childhood. Someday we will be rich and philanthropic. Or we will be poor but dedicated to science or to mission work. Or we will be famous for our writing, painting, or musicianship. At least we will have a family, a comfortable home, and some secure investments for retirement.

   I have not come across any studies that reveal how many people, by the age of forty, have reached their goals in life. My guess is that it would be few indeed. Realizing that they have not fulfilled their dreams by midlife can create the belief that they never will do so. This belief is most likely to precipitate the helplessness, hopelessness, and sadness that are major ingredients of depression.

2. *The Diagnostic and Statistical Manual of Mental Disorders,* 3rd ed. (American Psychiatric Association, 1980), p. 217.

3. *Children are becoming independent.* By forty, many couples have at least one child going off to college or out on his own or getting married. The fabled empty nest quickly becomes a reality at this age. And mothers seem to feel it more deeply than fathers, although both parents are aware of having spent too little time with the children. Fearful of having failed to teach them how to make it in life, parents feel that they have no time to recoup these losses.

4. *Many women experience serious midlife crises.* Women are uniquely conditioned by their physiological makeup and through childbearing to accept the inevitable limits of power and to be mature enough to function realistically within these limits. But that is not to say that they avoid crises.

5. *Lost opportunities become evident.* Several of my friends have not been able to be married and yet have yearned for that relationship. There are many reasons for such a fact, but for those who do not find their wish for marriage fulfilled, there is a strong sense of being deprived or even cheated.

   As these women pass their fortieth birthdays, they realize that not only have they missed out on the intimacy of marriage, but they are not likely to have children either. To those who have longed for these experiences, losing out on them is markedly depressing.

6. *Divorce may dash one's hopes.* Over the past several years I have shared with several women their heartache over divorce. On some occasions it was the wife who sought the divorce, the only logical choice to her. Nevertheless, these women may experience deep depression as they face life alone and give up their dreams of an idyllic old age shared by a lifelong companion.

7. *Ideals and values may change.* With so many opportunities for a career and the pleasure of being independent, a number of women have chosen to stay single. For some this proves a wise

choice and they find life rewarding. For others, the crises of the middle years create a new sense of loneliness and a longing for something else. They may regret their earlier decision and become depressed.

Actually, there is no category of women (or men) who are not vulnerable to a period of some degree of depression.

Women, in my experience, often become depressed during the menopause and grieve over their empty nests. But at least for some fifteen to twenty years, many of them begin to rediscover themselves. They often return to college, find jobs they once dreamed about, or become involved in worthwhile volunteer efforts.

Those who, tragically, lose husbands to other (and usually younger) women after several decades of marriage suffer multiplied anguish. When they are feeling their weakest and ugliest, losing that glorified "sex appeal," and wondering what they can possibly do with the rest of their lives, the men on whom they depended are gone.

I have shared the indescribable pain, anger, and helplessness these women experience. And I have marveled at the courage they find to rebuild their lives in successful ways. These examples remind me that there is always healing for grief and recovery from depression through courage, determination, and good decisions.

Influences from the Past

In the dramatic changes of midlife both the weaknesses and the strengths of the past will reemerge. How individuals handle this critical time will depend on the balance of these characteristics. Perhaps through the story of my own midlife stress I can exemplify this fact, and you may discover some facts about yourself. I believe each of us is uniquely an individual, but I have learned, to my comfort, that I have much in common with many others.

My early childhood was hardly blemished by sadness. I was the youngest of six children (three brothers and two sisters), well-loved by all of them, happy, and secure. A friend told me a few years ago that when he worked on the farm with my father, he enjoyed seeing me play. I loved to run to my dad and jump into his arms. One day Dad commented to this friend, "Ralph, she's the best example I know of abundant life!"

I was blessed with many relatives who were close to me when I was a child. I observed them having times of merriment and laughter, but I also saw various ones become morose, quiet, and irritable at times. Periodically, one aunt would come to visit, but she would hardly talk. Even now I can picture the drawn lines of her sad, depressed face.

During the stressful times of the economic depression of the 1930s, I observed my strong, teasing father, my adored hero, become withdrawn and silent; he had those same lines of care etched deeply in his face. I became quietly anxious over the change in him and hoped he would resume his teasing and laughter.

My grandmother lived with us, and occasionally other relatives spent some weeks or months in our home. For some years we were heavily burdened by financial hardships, and the stresses of meeting the needs of such a large family were great.

When I was sick, I received unusually tender and plentiful attention. I was subject to severe strep throats and would have to stay in bed for days at a time. Mother would find time to tell me stories and bring special foods on a tray, and Dad would even manage to sit with me in the evenings to read wonderful stories by the light of the kerosene lamp.

One major event disrupted the flow of my otherwise contented and happy life. When I was five, my baby sister was born. I had never needed a younger sister and was not told of her expected birth. Her arrival suddenly catapulted me out of my position as the beloved baby of the family. Overnight I became grief-stricken and wandered about my home, feeling abandoned and displaced by this truly adorable, charming child.

My mother, furthermore, failed to understand my situation and berated me for my displeasure. I felt guilty because I could not love my new sister, hurt and angry about my mother's scoldings, and confused and helpless over such an overwhelming happening.

Fortunately, the Creator who set life in motion also made it with a tendency to recover from pain and sickness. So I, too, eventually healed from the events that left me feeling rejected and undesirable. I learned again to play and laugh, study, work, and achieve. But I had scars that left me vulnerable. I cried easily, sought comfort where I could, and often felt sorry for myself.

My grandmother became my solace. She was quite a lady, and her life was one of the healthy parts of mine. A frail, bent woman with snow-white hair neatly coiled in a bun at the nape of her neck, she was totally deaf.

In her late twenties she had fallen in love with a fervent young evangelist. She moved from her extremely sheltered life in the heart of Pennsylvania to the plains of Kansas to marry him.

As she related the stories of her early years, I sensed with wonder the courage and quiet strength inside this small woman. She was left alone for weeks as Jacob rode on horseback to the many churches he helped to organize. He performed funerals, blessed marriages, and dedicated to God the children who were born. Always he taught the incomparable love and power of the God he had come to know so well.

Hannah mourned the loss of the child who died in infancy and then her dearly beloved husband who, at age forty, died after a short illness of meningitis. Truly alone, she raised their two sons and a daughter.

Never did I see my grandmother depressed. She learned to read lips quite well, and a tablet and pencil were always with her so we could write any message she could not understand. On one occasion she said to me, "I don't mind being deaf. I've never had to hear angry comments or dirty jokes. I just talk with Jesus." Her face with its increasing wrinkles settled into a calm, peaceful expression that rarely varied.

Whenever I felt especially misunderstood by my mother or siblings, I could find refuge in Grandma's room. At the foot of her tidily made bed was a folded comforter, the softest I have ever felt. I was welcome to bury my face in it and soak it with my childish tears whenever I needed to do so. Grandma never criticized me or my family. She simply sat in her chair, piecing her quilts and being the eye of my childhood storms.

The terror and tragedy of World War II involved our world and my brother during the years of my adolescence. The war also served as the background for some unsettling episodes in my life.

My sister and I had to live some distance from home so that we could attend high school. We certainly missed the warmth and intimacy of our big family.

Then when I was only sixteen, Grandma died. She simply slipped from her sleep to her long-lost Jacob and the Father they had so dearly loved and served. My comfort was gone.

Less than four months later, my father came to the home where my sister and I were staying. It was a stormy night with the loud thunder and crackling lightning that only Kansas can produce.

His face first revealed that some tragedy had occurred. As gently as he could, Dad told my sister and me that our youngest brother had suffered a terrible accident. In his haste to finish a task on the farm before the storm broke, he jerked a rope that was to close a huge hanging door on the barn. The rope broke, and the heavy door dropped, crushing him against the wall of the barn. He died instantly.

Together, our family grieved his loss. His subtle good humor, handsome face, and his integral part in our family were gone. As much as I missed the comfort of my elderly grandmother, the loss of this vital young brother, soon to become a father, was infinitely more painful.

But life had to go on, though we wished it would stop. We all worked harder to fill the gap his death had created. Healing again began its designated process.

Only six weeks went by before my father's sister became critically ill. Unable to have children of her own, she loved her nieces and nephews, and I loved the way she laughed. Her double chins and entire body would shake when something really funny became a topic of conversation.

Aunt Tillie had encephalitis. Even now this disease is highly fatal, and then it was almost certain death. After several days of unconsciousness, however, she began to rally. She had a brief period of seemingly normal functioning, but suddenly she died. The brain, so devastated by the infection, simply stopped working.

One more loss. Another episode of grief with its inherent anger, pain, helplessness, and futility.

Looking back, I can see the strongly polarized forces that formed my life. Mainly profound love and strength surrounded and penetrated my developing young personality.

But there were losses and heartaches that my sensitive spirit had to endure, even when I felt I simply could not.

My parents' religious beliefs became a powerful force in my life. To me, God was mainly loving, helpful, and forgiving. I learned in many ways how essential He was in my life.

On the other hand, my parents followed a narrow, strict life-style that separated me by light years from my peers. As I mentioned earlier, I had to abide by a rigid dress code. The parties and fun of my classmates were not to be for me. I could not skate, dance, or attend movies and most of the events that fill the social lives of teenagers. And yet I had to mingle with them, feeling monstrously strange.

I survived. And I even learned to compensate for my social "differentness" by becoming a top student, a good listener, and someone who could comfort others who hurt because I knew what pain was.

When I turned forty, I experienced a sense of restlessness. I was finding the stress of working, mothering, and being a wife, friend, and community volunteer simply unbearable.

I would awaken early with terrifying, angry dreams. Struggling to an upright posture, I would look at my soft, comfortable pillow, so reminiscent of my grandmother's comforter, and say to myself, "I'll get through this day, knowing my pillow will be here tonight." And I did get through my days. I loved my family and met their needs, cared for my patients with tenderness, and handled the management of my staff with some finesse.

In a teaching seminar, I finally had to acknowledge some basic facts. I did not like myself. Much of the heroic work I did was an unconscious attempt to prove to myself that I was not worthless. One of my father's oft-repeated, half-teasing questions to me as a child was, "Gracie, do you think you'll ever amount to anything?" I wasn't always sure what "amounting to anything" meant, but I assured Dad that I certainly would. And so I tried harder and harder to be perfect, strong, and pleasing to everyone. I was giving far more than I was receiving. And though the Bible clearly states it is more blessed to give, I now know that we also *must* receive (blessed or not!) or we become emotionally bankrupt.

I had to face it. I was approaching emotional bankruptcy. I was depressed, and I had feelings of anger, sadness, hopelessness, guilt, and helplessness. Well, not quite helplessness because I knew where to go for help. With a great sense of failure, I prayed for guidance, but my faith was weak. In retrospect I know my prayers were answered.

As I began weekly visits with a marvelous psychiatrist to whom God guided me, I began to fit together the pieces of my past. The strength that was part of the legacy of my grandparents and parents made me say, "I will *not* spend the rest of my life in despair." The trust that I learned to have in my parents and in my God allowed me to seek the help that was beyond my own strength. The determination that had pulled our family through the losses and grief of my youth held me on course as I worked with my psychiatrist.

I learned that I had far more strength than I had felt. I discovered that seeking help was not, as I had feared, a sign of weakness or failure; it was a sign of courage and honesty. I began to understand that the way to get loving attention was not through the extremes of helpless illness (as in my childhood sicknesses) nor in giving beyond my capacity to those who sought help from me.

The way to meet my needs was through admitting that I, the strong one, *had* needs, defining clearly what they were, and asking specifically for the supplying of those needs. It was both embarrassing and frightening to have to ask, but I took that risk. To my surprise, I found that many people were delighted to be asked and that my asking helped them.

About this time in the process, I fell and broke my ankle one icy winter day. My work was demanding, but I could not drive for a while. I called a list of friends to seek their services as driver for me until I could recover.

My friend, Ellen, hesitated just a bit when I called, but she gladly agreed to drive me downtown on a Friday. She seemed a bit nervous, but we chatted away as she skillfully maneuvered through the heavy morning traffic. I was so grateful to her. Later, Ellen confided she had gathered all her courage to do this labor of real love. She was terrified of driving in heavy traffic, but for me she heroically overcame her fear. Discovering that she *could* transcend her fear became a gateway to an entirely new growth spurt in her life. Knowing she cared enough for me to combat her fear made our friendship even more precious.

Another discovery I made was that of distinguishing grief from depression. As one by one my three children left home, first for college and then marriage, I felt exactly as I had during my depression. But I learned that grief is focused on a loss that is clearly defined and easily understood. Depression is not clear. It is a heavy mixture of emotions that hang over the individual like a shroud that cannot be shaken off. Knowing the phases of grief made it possible for me to get through that sadness and return to joyful living with greater speed.

A significant, life-changing fact I unearthed was that we have the gift of the power to choose. There are, of course, many differences between human beings, created in the image of God, and animals. But one of the most important is the ability to reason, to consider information and, on the basis of facts, to make choices. It took me a long time to understand that there are two levels of choice.

The first choice is that of deciding *how we will react* to things that happen to us. Dr. Victor Frankl, an inmate of the Nazi concentration camp, Auschwitz, wrote poignantly of the torture he and the other inmates endured. His very being was tormented by the cruelty of man to man, yet he refused to allow his spirit to be broken. He wrote and taught, after his release, that the ultimate power of humankind is to choose to remain loving, compassionate, and giving even when tormented and dehumanized.

The second choice, and for me much more difficult to comprehend, is that of deciding *how we will feel*. Choosing how we react can be mastered with willpower and self-discipline. But emotions hit us powerfully offside, as it were. Fear, hurt, anger, or excitement and joy can possess us unbidden. How, then, can we choose what we feel?

My own experience is this: I cannot prevent any emotion from welling up in me. The death of a friend causes the pain of grief. Facing serious financial problems prompts panic. Anticipating time with my grandson stimulates love and joy, which I obviously want to prolong.

When a negative, painful emotion assails me, here is what I do with it.

1. I allow its full impact to become clear to me, and I try to find the best name I can for it. At this stage, I do not try to avoid its pain.

2. Next I make sure that I understand what has caused the feeling. Sometimes it is an event that has happened today. Often it is a dim memory of crises from the past that may be like something that has occurred currently.

3. I think about the power I have, or do not have, in the situation producing my emotion. I put into effect what I can do in a carefully planned manner. I seek the help I may need to work out an answer. And then I let go of the things I cannot do.

4. If the feeling and problem are connected to a hurtful person over whom I have no influence, I work through a process of forgiving that person, and I choose to begin understanding and loving (as best I can) that difficult person.

5. If I am at fault in the problem, I clarify my mistakes, make such restitution as I can, and then forgive myself, learning to avoid that same wrongdoing again.

6. I prayerfully seek the infinite wisdom and love of God and choose to give Him control over me where my own resources would fail.

I am far from perfect in practicing these steps, but the more I remember to apply the principles, the better life becomes. And I have had occasion to test them out in some extremely difficult situations.

Signs and Symptoms

Depression in Middle-Aged Women

1. *Loss of interest* or pleasure in all or almost all usual activities and pastimes. They feel blue, sad, hopeless, or irritable and may look sad.

2. *Changes in eating, sleeping, and exercise* patterns from what has been normal.

3. *Loss of interest in sexual activity.*

4. *Loss of energy* and a sense of fatigue.

5. *Feelings of worthlessness,* self-reproach, or guilt.

6. *Difficulty in thinking* and concentrating and trouble in making decisions.

7. *Recurrent thoughts of death,* wishes to be dead, and suicidal thoughts or attempts.

8. *Tendency to focus on physical appearance* and functions. Preoccupation with even minor aches and pains.

Since learning how to practice this power of choice, I am aware that I need never be totally powerless. A big factor is thus removed from depression.

Having learned how to forgive, and having made a commitment to living in a state of forgiveness, I need not stay angry. Since anger *feels* deceptively powerful, it is tempting to want to stay a little bit angry—well, at least resentful! But as much as possible, I discipline myself to collect information, understand *why* another person did something hurtful, and then discipline myself to let go of all the anger and pain. Essentially, I stop making another person's problem mine. By giving up hurt and anger, I become free from another big ingredient of depression. By forgiving myself, making restitution, and seeking God's promised forgiveness, I am free from guilt.

The more I love, the less I fear. The Bible is concise that "perfect love casts out fear" (1 John 4:18). So you see, you can, as I am doing, learn to overcome depression. Simply consider each of its component emotions and work through them. You are welcome to use my steps in conquering depression or develop your own. You may be able to overcome it by yourself, or as I did, you may need the help of a trained therapist. I just want you to know there is hope.

7

Middle-Aged Men

"*What do you* know about electroshock treatment?" asked the taut voice on the telephone. Few comments or questions disarm me, but this one came close! It was not the question that troubled me, though; it was the obvious tension and stark anxiety accompanying it.

Briefly and as encouragingly as possible, I explained to this stranger about various therapies for depression. I promised to find for him the names of some physicians skilled in such therapy, hung up my phone, and resumed my efforts to clear the eternal stack of paper off my desk.

But my mind refused to focus on the facts relating to policy, programs, and the accreditation process for our hospital. To quiet my troubled mind, I found my finger tracing the caller's number, and I invited him to visit me in my office.

Soon I was confronting a giant of a man—gigantic in stature and also in honesty. He had not slept, he said, without sleeping pills for thirteen years. He had been on different kinds of medicine, and each in turn would lose its effect. He lived in dread of the imminent day when no more medications could be found to relieve his anguish and provide the slim solace of sleep.

Jim was a man of deep faith and equally profound doubts. Although he had a brilliant mind, he had spent at least a dozen years believing he was stupid. When he was in his midteens, a teacher spotted his superb intellect under the fading vestiges of a severe dyslexia (a condition that affects the ability to read). With her confidence in him, his achievements started to grow, and finally he believed in his abilities.

Jim's childhood was a history of troubled times. He was a twin and from birth lived in the shadow of his firstborn brother. The stress of that pregnancy and birth evidently made an invalid of their mother, and to this day, Jim's relatives remind him of the harm he did to her.

Jim and his brother were cared for by a hired nurse who also looked after the mother. His father worked long hours to provide for the family and had little energy left with which to love or enjoy the boys. He was, in fact, an austere man who rarely smiled, often punished, and never hugged his children.

The lack of freedom to run and play (understandable since the mother was never very well and demanded the boys stay in the house under her watchful eye) created a chronic frustration and depression during Jim's early years. He would see other children out of doors, and he would nearly become wild when he would hear the huge locomotives roar over a nearby trestle. He knows now his mother was trying to protect him, but then he yearned to run and feel the wind in his ears, have the rain tickle his nose, and see the train whose whistle enchanted him.

As he grew up, Jim feared a God whom he believed to be as severe as his father. Yet someone must have planted a tiny seed of hope that He was something more. Jim's immensely mixed feelings trapped him in adult depression that was almost incapacitating.

At a point when Jim believed his child might have a fatal disease, his emotions broke. The austere, punishing father of his childhood became, to him, a huge, merciless, vengeful God who was about to perform the ultimate punishment. In retribution for his doubts, confusion, and imagined failures, Jim believed God would take his beloved child.

As in the lives of Isaac and Abraham of old, the threatened sacrifice was not required. Jim's child did not have a fatal illness after all, and she was well. Then Jim believed he was ill. He would weep in agony over his helplessness and worthlessness. But that core of health held steady, and he could always manage to go to work. Among people he could function in a highly credible fashion.

Various physicians treated Jim with and without medication, with psychotherapy, and with encouragement. And with immeasurable slowness, he inched his way back to a ray of hope. His call to me was a desperate search for a miracle that might suddenly recapture his earlier era of success and excitement. He wanted to be rid of the extreme fear of failure of his early years and relive the joy of his high school era when he discovered he could succeed.

In a recent episode of despondency, Jim penned these words. They say how he often feels.

Dawn

It is the pain, all day, every day. It is having a clear mind to fully endure painful emotion. It is the time involved now. The five years of this battle. Every morning, the pensive sharp points of pain stab like daggers of ice. They melt to a point, and the point remains all day. I try to relate this all to my past, a long time ago, knowing that if I can connect wires of now to terminals of then, current will flow, creating a circuit and thus stopping the snapping loose ends of short-circuited suffering.

The fear is twenty or more years of this. Seven or eight thousand more mornings of pilled, drugged wakeups. Then the day, the performance, the night of relief, the morning of jagged, renewed agony.

Is this my battle? If so, God, steady my hands so that I may strap on the armour.

Since that first visit, Jim has continued to stretch painfully for patience; he has grown toward health in remarkable degrees. And he still backslides to near despair at times. He is taking a new medication that eases his tension, and that is wise. One day, perhaps soon, Jim will realize that he can choose how he will feel. This will never be as easy as deciding how he will act when he goes to work, but it will come!

In many ways Jim's story is unique, but it also is the same as that of untold numbers of men. Fortunately (though Jim doesn't yet agree that it is fortunate), he had enough stress and that finely tuned balance in vulnerability and strength to admit his problem. It was undeniable. It overwhelmed him. And it demanded that he get help. But many depressed men refuse to feel their pain. They deny it instead. They will not ask for the help they so badly need and thereby both perpetuate and aggravate their pain.

Melvin was one man who would never admit he was less than "terrific!" When anyone asked him how he was, that was uniformly his answer. Rarely, if ever, would he admit to being just "okay" or even "fine." I always suspected that he didn't really feel that great but was like the anxious boy, afraid of the dark, who whistled to bolster his spirits. And I must say, I have great respect for a person who faces the dark with courage like Melvin expressed.

There were, however, problems in his philosophy. The problems slowly and relentlessly sneaked up on him when events in his life turned sour. When he suffered the loss of loved ones in death, Melvin comforted his comforters. When business failures caused debts to mount, he refused to believe times were economically bad. Things would be better tomorrow. When his children grew up and left home, he refused to mourn the emptiness. He was always glad they could be independent. There was a truly commendable quality in Mel's optimism and expressed confidence.

His problems lay in two areas—one was his denial of reality and the other was his adamant refusal to accept advice, comfort, or support. Men (especially Melvin) were supposed to be strong, to take their lumps, to get up and get going again. His policies had always worked before; they would continue to succeed. But Melvin's stresses outgrew his philosophy.

In medical school, I learned that everyone has a breaking point. Mentally, emotionally, or physically when stress reaches that point, some part of the individual will give way. And so it happened to Melvin. He became emotionally broken—depressed. Even at the breaking point he could not admit his desperation, and he refused both help and comfort. His attitudes and actions were such that his wife could no longer put up with him, and she obtained a separation.

The contrast between Jim and Melvin is very small at the beginning of their stories. Both felt stress, though of somewhat varying sorts. Both wanted to handle it themselves, but Jim admitted he couldn't cope and found help. Melvin never could accept his limitations, and he rejected any of the help that could have saved his marriage and, perhaps at some point, even his business.

A biblical paradox states that we are strong only when we are weak (2 Corinthians 12:10), and through the experiences of life, I have come to understand that. Had Melvin admitted he was weak in some areas, he could have sought and used the advice and comfort he needed. He then would have grown in his perceptions, knowledge, and relationships. He would indeed have become strong.

Through Jim's extreme stress, he had no choice. Help beyond himself was unavoidable. And through that help he has become much wiser, stronger, and more successful.

As I discussed in the previous chapter, many men go through a midlife crisis because they have a difficult time accepting the inevitability of aging and its effects on them physically. Their deep-down depression makes some men go to great lengths to prove themselves youthful and virile. It is not unusual for some of them to seek a younger wife. Others push themselves harder and harder on the job, becoming workaholics.

Men, whether your depression at midlife comes from the inevitability of your aging, the loss of loved ones, business disasters, or the global uncertainties we all face, there is hope for you! Here is all you have to do:

- Be honest enough with yourself to admit that your stress is too great to handle alone.

- Be self-aware enough to recognize the immensity of your emotional and physical strain in reaction to that stress; face your depression.

- Be strong enough to admit that you have a weak spot or two. (It really takes a fairly secure man to face this fact.)

- Be wise enough to seek out the best type of help for you—your wife's comfort, your adult child's confidence, your pastor's spiritual counsel, or professional advice.

- Be tenacious enough to follow through with these steps and your chosen help until your depression is over.

A Word to the Wives!

Perhaps some of you are fortunate enough to have a husband who is open to your strength, can accept your help without a sense of inferiority, and has learned direct, open, and honest communication. If so, read no further. You will be able to help him out rather readily.

However, if your husband has certain weaknesses he cannot admit, you will profit from some guidance. Perhaps these suggestions can help:

- Acquire all the information you can about your husband's situation. Ask him; tactfully ask a partner or friend or anyone who may be aware of his problems.

- Read his body language. When you see a sad or worried face, catch a dejected posture, or find his eating or sleeping habits changing, seek a place and time to talk with him, but do not badger him.

- Speak the truth in love. Avoid anxiety, anger, or blame. Simply tell him what you see in him, that you know he is under grave stress, and that you love him and want to help him.

- Ask him what he needs and how you can be of the greatest help. (Do not believe him when he replies, "Just leave me alone!")

- Have, at your fingertips, a few choice resources that he may call upon privately—a skilled counselor, a pastor, or a person who is skilled in the area of his problem. Give this information to him, kiss him, and give him time to think alone.

SIGNS AND SYMPTOMS

Depression in Middle-Aged Men

1. *Loss of interest* or pleasure in all or almost all usual activities and pastimes. They feel blue, sad, hopeless, or irritable and may look sad.

2. *Changes in eating, sleeping, and exercise* patterns from what has been normal.

3. *Loss of interest in sexual activity.*

4. *Loss of energy* and a sense of fatigue.

5. *Feelings of worthlessness,* self-reproach, or guilt.

6. *Difficulty in thinking* and concentrating and trouble in making decisions.

7. *Recurrent thoughts of death,* wishes to be dead, and suicidal thoughts or attempts.

8. *Tendency to focus on physical appearance* and functions. Preoccupation with even minor aches and pains.

- *Do not nag him.*

- From time to time, offer him extra encouragement, support, or whatever your most loving intuition dictates.

- Rarely, with objective, professional advice, you may need to practice "tough love" with an extra-stubborn man. Forget for a bit any beliefs about your role as a submissive wife, and insist that he seek professional help. Go with him if you need further help in knowing how to assist him, or go alone for guidance that could save needless heartache.

- During any time of excess stress, be as little trouble to your spouse as possible. Ask for as few bits of help as possible. Spend no money you don't have to; avoid time and social demands when he especially needs rest, but keep him active and help him find healthy escapes.

Most of us grow the best through our darkest days and most traumatic events. Therefore, I will not wish for you a life free of trouble and depression. I do, however, wish for both husbands and wives to give and receive the sort of support and guidance that only tested love can offer.

8

Older
People

After middle age comes the relentless approach of old age. Further physical changes are taking their toll, hastening the appearance and functional limitations of the aging process.

Just when old age begins is difficult to define. All of us know people who seem old at forty and those who appear exuberantly young at eighty. Generally speaking, however, old age begins at the point of retirement. Senior status is given those who are fifty-five or older, according to the American Association of Retired Persons (AARP).

Early in this process people must retire—often without having attained the anticipated success or fulfilled dreams of their youth. The realization that they are now unlikely to ever reach those goals can create pockets of helplessness and despair.

As in youths who are depressed, life may seem unbearable, and suicide becomes common. According to the 1986 *Annual Report of Vital Statistics,*[1] there are 38.9 suicides per 100,000 population

---

1. U.S. National Center for Health Statistics, *Vital Statistics of the United States*, Annual, 1986, Table No. 122.

among white men sixty-five and over. In white women this figure is 6.5. And among blacks, these figures are 12.4 men and only 1.8 women per 100,000. Perhaps white women and minorities learn better than white men how to accept their finiteness.

The signs and symptoms of depression in older people are identical with those given for young adults and new parents. However, these symptoms are commonly overlooked as being part of senility. There is little effort to provide psychotherapy, and not much is done to offer the best quality of life possible for the aged. Such efforts are costly, and after all, they won't live too much longer anyway. At least these seem to be the beliefs of many nursing homes or other long-term care facilities where older people are relegated in our Western culture. And even the devoted families who try to care for the elderly in their homes may be ill-prepared to cope with those who suffer from depression.

Certainly we have no easy answers for the growing problem of providing care for the aged. Our society needs to "brainstorm" some better solutions than we now know!

Depression in Older People

I recently passed my sixty-first birthday, and like many other people, I want to deny my senior citizen status. When I receive mail from the AARP, I want to trash it at once. Even when I realize I'm entitled to financial discounts here and there because of my age, I resist revealing my entitlement.

Actually, I doubt my resistance to aging has to do with pride or how people may feel toward me as I grow old. I believe it has to do with facing encroaching disabilities that are inevitable. I am the most fortunate older woman I know. I have an exciting job, many precious friends, a family who could not possibly be more supportive and loving, and excellent health. I have so many hobbies and interests that I look forward to retirement when I will have time to pursue them.

Yet with regularity I find new wrinkles in my skin, added aches and stiffness in my body, and a greater reluctance to cope with new gadgets. I have experienced some of the condescension of the young to us older citizens. I don't like any of these facts about myself or others, and I struggle to transcend them or deny them.

Currently, I am working with my attorney to write a new will. As I was reading it, I found myself thinking, ridiculously, of the ways I would help my children execute it. Like being hit by a bolt of lightning, I suddenly realized that when it came time to put that will to use, I would no longer be present to help my children care for last-minute business details. I faced, at that moment, the universally ultimate position of helplessness, my own death.

For just a few minutes, a sense of depression that was largely grief assailed me. I love living, I enjoy my dearest friends who are my family, and I do not relish the idea of losing them. I do not want to die. But I have no control over the fact that I will die. I suspect that it is the loss of control we all dread more than death itself. I do not want to lose my mobility, vision, or hearing. Above all, I do not want to lose my ability to think, learn, and communicate. But I have no control over the possibility of these losses.

Through reviewing my faith and philosophy of life I was able, rather soon, to regain my emotional equilibrium. I shed a few egotistical but loving tears for those who will grieve over losing me, and then I made the best decision I knew how to make. I will take care of myself the very best I can to maintain optimal health, energy, and independent functioning as long as possible. I will practice love, commitment, and honesty and will give as much of whatever is good about me to as many people as I can. And when I no longer can control my life successfully, I will trust someone to care about me enough to provide the structure and help I will need. You see, I do practice the philosophies I share, and they work!

Losses

Each era of life has its unique losses and grief. Certainly, that is true of the elderly. Men are evidently particularly susceptible to despair in their old age, a fact indicated by the suicide rates cited earlier. The types of losses of older people are easily listed, but coping with them is much more difficult.

1. *Loss of productivity.* For men and women who have gained a significant part of their identities from their jobs, this loss is catastrophic. Having no measurable results at the end of the day to prove their worth can indeed be depressing if they have depended on such proof of their value for self-esteem. Frankly, I believe this is more problematic for men than for women, who usually have a broader basis for valuing themselves.

2. *Loss of physical assets.* The physical attractiveness of youth is lost, and there is an inevitable progression in the decline of the senses as well as neuromuscular functions. Sight, hearing, taste, smell, movement, and involuntary control of bladder and bowel action decrease with age. Obviously, these degenerative changes vary from one person to another, but they will take place. In some elderly people sexual activity is lost with all the enjoyment this has afforded them. Trying to bathe can become a challenge, and taking a trip to a shopping center alone is truly impossible for some.

3. *Social and personal losses.* A number of my medical school classmates are no longer alive, and each class reunion reminds us of our finiteness. Each of us secretly wonders who will be missing five years hence. Of course, we believe it will not be us! With each advancing year, more and more of our peers will die. If we allow it, we can enter into a sense of despair at the futility of waiting for our own demise.

    In every retirement center there are residents who have absolutely no living relatives. I cannot imagine the frightening loneliness of such a state. Unless older singles have carefully cultivated loyal friends, they are likely to not only feel, but *be,* abandoned. If poverty complicates the loneliness, true desperation must be the case.

    Those who lose a spouse are truly susceptible to depression as well as grief. Often the couples who have been longtime friends feel uneasy with this person who is a reminder of the inevitability of their own deaths and loss, and they do not want to face that. Social functioning, especially for women, becomes limited to family and other widowed people. Thankfully, senior citizen groups in most communities have alleviated this loneliness.

4. *Cultural devaluation.* In Eastern cultures, older people are revered, and great care is lavished on them. Not so in many parts of the Western world. In the United States most elderly people are relegated to old folks' homes or nursing centers. Among my acquaintances I can think of only a handful of families who have taken into their homes a grandparent or other relative who could not remain independent.

   I am working on a series of plans that will avoid my becoming a burden to my children. And they tell me they would be happy to take care of me if and when I need that help. Our society has made us believe that we should not have to endure the inconvenience of waiting on those who become unable to function on their own. My grandmother lived with my family for many years, and her presence enriched my life. Perhaps as a culture, we need to review our values and renew a commitment to elderly family members.

5. *Loss of financial stability.* Prior to retirement, people have some financial options. They can earn promotions or seek new positions to enhance their incomes. Working a second job can tide a family through financial crises. Even borrowing money can be an option. Few, if any, of these possibilities exist for older people. If they can find part-time work at all, their income must be extremely limited, or they lose their Social Security benefits. Jobs for them are almost nonexistent. Even people in their fifties are often passed over in the job market. Yet the costs of living continue to rise, and from time to time, inflation makes it impossible to budget successfully a moderate fixed income.

6. *Loss of familiar environment.* As people grow older, the security of the familiar becomes self-evident. Despite the increasing

stress of maintaining my own home, I plan to keep living there as long as I possibly can. It holds my memories, my comfortable furniture, the pictures that express my personality, and even some of the treasures from the home of my birth.

As the elderly become unable to manage their own homes, they often are forced to move to new, unfamiliar places. They reach for a light switch, and it isn't there. At night they become confused trying to find the bathroom and may even have an accident. The door is simply not where it should be.

Changes are difficult at best. For the elderly with the habits of years deeply etched in them, changes become almost impossible. Unless you are able to provide some personal help, I urge you not to move or have your aged parents move to a new place of residence until that is absolutely necessary.

7. *Loss of spiritual resources*. This loss is by no means universal. As my grandmother and parents reached old age, their faith grew in its certainty, and the God they had served became increasingly real to each of them.

On the other hand, some elderly people of previously strong belief reveal the feeling that God is far away. They cannot believe that He would allow them to go through so much pain or face such extreme helplessness. They may even take their lives because of the hopelessness of their despair.

There are several reasons for the loss of faith in old age. Many people see God only as a conveyor of good things. They have been blessed with basically comfortable lives and perhaps do not understand the cycles of health and sickness, prosperity and reverses, and life and death. Certainly their statements would suggest their misconceptions of God. Some people have given only a superficial allegiance to God and have not taken time to learn much about Him. Many elderly suffer enough degeneration of their minds that their earlier ability to trust and love God is lost. People with organic brain damage often cannot identify their own children and friends. It stands to reason, then, that they would be unable to recognize their relationship with God, no matter how closely they have walked beside Him.

In older people, who are at a low ebb in their energy and general functioning, these losses are magnified, and their grief is intense. Collectively the depression that occurs is so marked that it is no wonder some take their own lives; suicide may appear to be the only means left to them of exerting some power or control.

Coping with Depression in Older People

Let's look at these losses and see what can be done to alleviate the depression associated with them.

1. *Loss of productivity.* If you have not yet retired, start preparing for that time by developing an old hobby or a special interest you may have. Do not pursue an area that will enslave you to such hard work that you find it laborious.

   If you have already retired, look for any area of usefulness that appeals to you and get involved in it. Volunteers are needed in many places. There are centers to teach almost any skill to fit your expertise. Whatever your preference, follow it. Allow plenty of time for resting, relaxing, traveling, fishing, or doing nothing. But let each week find a list of accomplishments with your signature on them!

2. *Loss of physical assets.* Many of the degenerative processes of old age cannot be prevented or cured, and in that fact lie great fear and grief. However, you can do some things to take care of yourself and both prolong and improve your quality of life.

   • *Eat properly.* Get the advice of a good nutritionist or dietitian. Your doctor's office, hospital, or telephone directory can help you locate one. Or look in your library or bookstore for the information you need to eat the best diet possible. Generally, a good multiple vitamin is a recommended supplement to the best of diets, but check this out with your doctor to be sure it's okay.

   • *Have a careful checkup* by your doctor twice a year. If she feels once a year is enough, follow that recommendation, but most of us should take the precaution of semiannual check-ups. Have your eyes checked regularly. Many visual problems are correctable with relatively simple surgical procedures. Hearing problems are so annoying. I can attest to that! Several people lately have told me they were told hearing aids would not help, but when they tried them, they heard much better. So give a hearing aid a chance.

- *Follow your doctor's recommendations.* Fairly often, I hear elderly people say, "I just don't like to take pills, so I don't." Or "I don't think living is worth it if I can't eat what I want!" Certainly no one likes to live with these restrictions, but doing so anyway can make the quality of your life much better.

- Take walks daily when the weather permits, and *stay* as *active* as you can. Balance activities with rest to receive the most benefit.

- *Try not to let sleep patterns become a problem.* Many of us do not need as much sleep when we grow older, but be certain any sleep disturbances are not a sign of the depression that can slip up on you. Avoid sleeping too frequently during the day. A number of catnaps can rob you of a night's sleep and make you worry about insomnia.

3. *Social and personal losses.* You have only two choices regarding the death of friends and relatives: you can become pessimistic and depressed about them and your own demise; or you can grieve their loss, relish your good memories of them, and give your attention to making your own life the best possible.

    If you are missing out on social events because you are now widowed, develop a new life-style. Join a senior citizens' group; look for other lonely people and set up times with selected ones. Seek out young families, far from their own grandparents, and develop a friendship. You will need to set your own limits on this sort of relationship, but it can benefit both you and the adopted family.

    Find a church if you haven't already, and become active in

its programs. Different interest groups may attract you. Find out what is available in your area. If there is nothing that appeals to you, find a few other people and begin your own group.

4. *Cultural devaluation.* All of us must learn to speak out about people's attitudes that are not right. Whether you enlighten only your own neighbors and relatives or large groups you have a responsibility to be heard.

Beyond your best efforts to change others' ideas and attitudes lies your own special power—the strength that enables you to know your assets so clearly that no one can rob you of them. You can avoid taking the put-downs of the elderly personally and develop your inner strength all the more!

5. *Loss of financial stability.* Many older people worry needlessly about money. Their resources are adequate, but they imagine all the dismal things that *could* happen and then react to their worry. On the other extreme are those who blissfully trust everything will be just fine, and they spend money as if they had an endless supply.

Somewhere in the middle of these extremes are the realists who budget carefully, restrict their spending, and find they can make it. I urge most older people to consult with a reliable financial counselor to ensure the safety of investments and to ascertain what retirement benefits they are entitled to receive.

One friend of mine, nearly eighty, has become so informed about financial matters that she has taught her teenage neighbor a great deal. I consider that excellent. She has a hobby, sharing with her neighbors enriches her social life, and she has increased her retirement income by careful management.

Be sure to look for and use the many gracious senior citizens' discounts and benefits that are available. And every time you save money you might have had to spend, stick it in a piggy bank or a savings account. You can actually create a bit of added security, and it can be fun to see what you can save.

Many elderly people must live on extremely limited retirement incomes or even on welfare. Make a tour of your neighborhood to see if there are added areas of assistance through churches or community agencies that can help you stretch your income.

Depression in Older People

1. *Loss of interest* or pleasure in all or almost all usual activities and pastimes. They feel blue, sad, hopeless, or irritable and may look sad.

2. *Changes in dietary patterns,* such as poor appetite and weight loss (without planned dieting) or increased appetite and weight gain.

3. *Sleep disturbances* characterized by lack of sleep or too much sleep.

4. *Changes in level of activity* resulting in hyperactivity (restlessness) or unaccustomed inactivity.

5. *Loss of interest in sexual activity.*

6. *Loss of energy* and a feeling of fatigue.

7. *Feelings of worthlessness,* self-reproach, or guilt.

8. *Difficulty in thinking* and concentrating and trouble in making decisions.

---

6. *Loss of familiar environment.* Recently I heard of a grandmother who decided to sell her belongings and move to a retirement home. Her children realized that she could no longer live alone and were grateful that she had chosen on her own to give up the responsibilities she carried and take it easy. She kept few of her personal items and did not even display the familiar photos of her family. She became markedly depressed, and her relationship with her family suffered because she did not communicate her sadness or mourning over losing her home. She martyrishly suffered her pain by withdrawing from them.

By contrast, my mother-in-law selected her most treasured pieces of furniture and bric-a-brac. She arranged them tastefully in her room at the retirement center she chose. Pictures of her dearest friends and family were conveniently placed so she could think fondly of them every day. And the time she spent with her family was full of warmth and good humor.

7. *Loss of spiritual resources.* I urge all older people to budget their time to allow for meditation, prayers, and reading. My brother recently told me he reads a portion of the Bible every day and plans to reread it every year. Many excellent books on spiritual issues are available to enrich your life. You may find peace of mind by such reading as I have. As you discover more and more about how big and loving God really is, I hope your faith will grow and your spirit will expand.

When I was in high school, I was required to memorize certain poems. One that I recall vividly was "The Chambered Nautilus." It describes a special seashell that contains sections of increasing size. As the little creature that lives in the shell grows, the shell must expand to accommodate the larger life. The lines I love are these:

> Let each new temple,
> Nobler than the last,
> Shut thee from heaven
> With a dome more vast,
> Till thou at length art free,
> Leaving thine outgrown shell
> By life's unresting sea!

SPECIAL FACTORS IN DEPRESSION

The best-seller *Megatrends* depicts the actual existence of the mechanized, computerized world of *1984*. The author wisely counsels, "We must become high touch [people] as we become more high tech."[1] But he does not tell us how to become such people. In desperation, I believe, many people seek the satisfaction of that universal need for touch through scintillating sexual experiences, only to find that recreational sex, too, results in loneliness and disappointment.

Many familial and cultural forces have been blamed for the problems of today's world. It is difficult to determine a single cause, but a common denominator is depression. And among its manifestations are problems associated with loneliness, seasonal changes, sexual dysfunction, disability and illness, religion, and grief. Surprisingly, perhaps, depression often brings its own fringe benefits.

---

1. John Naisbitt, *Megatrends* (New York: Warner Books, Inc., 1982), p. 45.

9

Loneliness

The sadness of older persons who are all alone is far too common. But loneliness is not restricted to any age group. Among the teeming millions in every metropolis there are uncounted lonely people. In poor tenements or luxury apartments, tiny homes or mansions, there are people who suffer from the depression of loneliness. Sometimes they have not learned how to reach out and connect with others. Many are afraid and suspicious. But often the growing self-centeredness of our society creates seemingly insurmountable barriers.

The United States Census Bureau reveals some startling facts. In 1960 about 4.5 million women were living alone, but in 1985 there were nearly 13 million.

Many women, abandoned by their husbands, raise one or more children alone. (About one white family out of six exists with a single mom.) Children alleviate the loneliness, but their needs add stress to mothers who crave the help and intimacy of adults. Many single mothers live away from their own families and find little support from them.

Among American blacks, nearly one out of two households is headed by a single woman. Often with dependency on low-paying jobs or inadequate welfare assistance, these stressed families almost inevitably face multiple levels of depression.

Adolescent Girls

Thirteen-year-old Sandy sat on my examining table as I listened to her heart and lungs. As my shiny stethoscope moved over her chest to check out breathing sounds, I heard words instead. Patiently, I removed the instrument from my ears so I could understand her.

Sandy said, "I can't wait for you to check my tummy. I hope you'll find I'm pregnant!" Few things startle me anymore, but most thirteen-year-olds do not frankly wish themselves pregnant!

I realized the physical examination would just have to wait as I asked her gently to explain why she would like to be pregnant. She certainly had the answer.

"You see, Dr. K.," she explained, "me and my parents don't get along so very good. They're always wantin' me to do something, and I don't like to be bossed around." She popped her bubble gum and continued, "Well, I had this dog, and he was so cute! But I wouldn't take very good care of him, see, and so Mom told me if I didn't start bein' responsible, they'd get rid of him. But, see, I didn't really believe 'em, so I never took very good care of him. But I did like him a lot. Well, they did get rid of him! And I miss him so much. So I ran away with this guy, see, and we had sex. 'Cause I just thought if I had a baby, they couldn't take it away from me. They couldn't, could they?" Her eyes showed panic.

Sandy, a bit younger than many teenage mothers, spoke clearly for many of them. She and they are so lonely, so depressed. They think if they had a child to love them, to *belong* to them, they would no longer be lonely. They become happy, even excited, about the prospect of having a child. But those feelings can change drastically when they are faced with the realities of the situation.

Today, nearly one out of ten girls will be pregnant before finishing high school. Many will sear their hearts by having an abortion. Others will have the child and try to nurture and care for it. But since babies need *so* much and give so little, these young moms will burn out in awhile. The more fortunate ones get help from parents or friends; others severely neglect those babies while trying to meet their own needs; and still others seriously abuse those helpless babies who failed to meet their needs.

Tragically, nearly 80 percent of teens who become pregnant early in high school will have another child before finishing school. And many never complete the education they so sorely need if they are to become mature, independent adults.

As you can see, the cost of loneliness, depression, and a poor self-image is extremely high. That cost in wasted potential, poorly parented youngsters (because *their* parents are still youngsters!), and the limited future they face is truly immeasurable.

Young Women

For some twenty years I have been closely involved with groups trying to prevent the tragic problems of teenage pregnancy. I know that many teens and young women in their early twenties become sexually active in an attempt to relieve their loneliness.

A college junior who was alone and expecting her first child described her life to me. A beautiful, intelligent girl, she sat in my study with tears soaking her stomach, swollen with her unborn child. Her father was an alcoholic who was seldom there for his wife or children. He never shared the excitement of the young actors in school plays or the winners of a baseball game. Nor was he there to console the losers or to give them the caring they craved. Her mother was loving and tried to make up to the children their loss of a loving father. But Kelly really needed her dad.

Away at college, she felt for the first time free of the anguishing struggles of her alcoholic family. But the inner emptiness, the loneliness, was achingly still there—until she met Kirk. He was all she could ever have dreamed. He was a good, if not brilliant, student, handsome in a strong, rugged way, socially confident, and in love with her.

It was easy for lonely, depressed Kelly to invite Kirk into her apartment. They would "pretend" they were married and had newly set up housekeeping. Kelly's eyes brightened as she remembered those early days of their relationship. There was someone fun to come home to—a man who cared about her day, her exams, her grades, and her anecdotes of her part-time job as a waitress. He would massage her aching feet, kiss her, and occasionally have dinner ready. It was fun to play house.

Kelly commented that she had never really enjoyed their sexual intimacy. But it was so neat, she confided, to awaken in the morning to find someone's arms around her—to *not* be alone!

Before the end of her junior year, their first semester together, Kelly found herself pregnant. At first she was horrified, wondering how she would finish college and what she would do for money and child care. *But,* she thought, *Kirk and I can manage anything. He's so strong and capable, and we're so much in love.*

All too soon, Kelly was catapulted back into her lifelong pattern of loneliness. It seemed Kirk had not counted on a child. He was not "into" marriage, had no money, and suggested she see an abortionist. Kirk was gone when Kelly returned from classes the day after she revealed her pregnancy. Kelly was alone.

But she was not quite alone, for inside her was a little person, daily growing bigger, getting ready to be born. Rarely have I shared the depths of despair that I sensed in Kelly. She wanted the child so that she would never again be alone. But she knew that yearning was largely self-centered and that she was in no way ready to be a parent. With the most heroic, altruistic love I have ever seen, Kelly finally decided to release her baby girl for adoption. And she, so much wiser, began to set goals for mending her grief, overcoming her depression, and finding a way to make her world a better place.

Many of today's singles think they have found the answers to depression. Nightly visits to bars, a few alcoholic drinks, a quick acquaintance, and an even quicker trip to someone's bed. No need for a commitment, no risks of further abandonments, no pain (or not much, at least). But they are truly deceiving themselves.

Single Men

Not only women, however, are alone and depressed. As a romantic Western culture, we tend to believe that men are more able to reach out and find companionship than are women. After all, they are, historically, the aggressors. But that is not always the case. Desperately lonely women are increasingly taking the initiative. They seek out and respond to men who seem to have intelligence, good looks and, above all, money. Many men tell me they regularly are propositioned by women they meet or work with.

But many men want more than recreational sex and quick propositions. They crave a lasting relationship, but they, too, have been rejected and suffered abandonment. So they are afraid either to seek or to respond to a woman and instead resort to superficial experiences.

A friend has permitted me to share his profound experiences of loneliness and depression. He writes:

> *My depression usually came on when I was lonely. I could be in a crowd of people and still be lonely.* [Not, may I add, an unusual experience.] *I had no one to pay attention to just me. Most of the time, in fact, I realized I could feel lonely and rejected by both my peers and my family.*
>
> *I finally discovered how to get myself out of feeling lonely. I would find someone—it mattered little who, where, or when—to have sex with. That became a false ''high'' that would pull me out of my low feeling.*
>
> *Even when I knew it was wrong, if I could touch someone or she would touch me, I felt better. If she would hug me, I felt even better—safe and loved—even for a moment!*
>
> *My father drank too much and spent most of his money on this habit. Our family was poor and I felt ashamed—as if I had to hide their failures. I didn't want anyone to know about my dad. I always wanted to feel important, to amount to something.*
>
> *When I grew up I joined many civic organizations. Most of this, for me, was just to feel important. I often was elected to an office and became a leader in these groups. If I could not achieve such a spotlighted position in a short time, I*

would drop my membership and seek a new group that would appreciate my talents. I wanted to be the best at something. I had great confidence in what I could do if I were given the chance.

However, I often used my talents in the wrong way. I tried to manipulate people to get what I wanted. When I couldn't, I would feel depressed, and then I would spend money or find someone to have sex with. Temporarily, I would feel good, "high," and escape my depression and loneliness.

I grew to know where to find a willing partner, a "quickie" hug or kiss, a brief relationship. I grew to avoid lasting relationships because I learned it was the conquest that made me feel excited, wanted, and good.

Finally I realized this high was false because I would feel satisfied for only a short time and then I would become restless, and seek a new experience. . . .

Even when I learned that God was the only One who can break this feeling, this vicious cycle, I found it difficult to trust Him. I've never found anyone I can trust. How can a person, deep in depression, turn to Him and ask for help?

This deeply personal, honest revelation describes clearly one of the causes and the experiences of a lonely, depressed person. Those of us who have found the security of lasting commitments with trustworthy loved ones must find new ways to reach out to those who have not.

Incompatible Marriage Partners

Karen is a mother of three children who are junior- and senior-high school students. She stands tall and erect, a study in dignity and poise that was etched through the pain of loneliness and depression.

Only a few years after the birth of their first child, Joy, Karen learned that her husband was having an affair. With the increasing frequency of such sordid behavior and its widespread advertisement through the media, perhaps our society has become calloused toward affairs. But a decade ago that was not the case.

Karen was hurt and angry. She desperately tried to win back her husband's loyalty and love. And she was successful. After occasional short flirtations, he renewed his commitment both to Karen and to God. He resumed steady work in his profession and activities in his church.

A few years later, however, Jim again began to wander away from Karen and his faith. His time with the family dwindled, and Karen became aware of the familiar old feeling of his not being there, even when his body was. By now she knew the pattern well and soon discovered his new romance.

As we talked together regularly, I sensed a new definition of loneliness. Karen lived with Jim, but his heart was not with her. His main emotional focus and energy were with his girlfriend, not his wife. She was lonely in his presence, trapped away from friends and family by her commitment to him and her efforts to win back his love.

After some long months of dedicated efforts, Karen began to face the facts. This man had some serious character flaws that were unlikely to be remedied since he was totally unwilling to face them.

The friend who allowed me to use his letter to describe his loneliness mentioned the contrast of being lonely in a crowd. It is possible to be equally lonely in the supposed intimacy of a marriage. When an individual cannot give or is unable to receive genuine love, substitutes are likely to be instituted. If only one partner is unable to exchange love, the other is left terribly lonely. Helplessness becomes apparent when every effort to effect change fails. Anger toward the spouse, at personal limitations, and at the hopelessness of the relationship is bound to ensue. Often the partner who suffers blames poor judgment or inadequate knowledge for the failure, so guilt increases. The sadness of it all can become overwhelming. Once again, the ingredients of depression are there, stemming from the loneliness of incompatibility.

Single Mothers

Susan, trim, well-groomed, and friendly, met me for lunch to share her experiences as a single mom of some ten years. Without much warning her husband abandoned her and their two sons, who were about two and five years of age.

As she reminisced about the struggles of those years, her bright eyes softened, but no tears appeared. She had finally overcome the depression of that era. One of the most difficult times she recalled was the ride to and from work. She would force herself to act cheerful for her children, and at work she could forget her pain and concentrate on her tasks. But with another adult who drove the car, she could close her eyes and concentrate for a few moments on herself. Susan recalled both the pain and the luxury of silence. She felt totally incapable of speaking and was grateful for the friend who understood her withdrawal—so typical of depression.

As her energetic sons grew, she was often acutely aware of the need for a sounding board. Many times she felt unsure of her disciplinary actions and her judgments. She yearned for an adult who could say, "That's okay," or simply, "You're okay!" There was no one to soften the hardness of her angry lectures or to toughen the consequences that she was at times too tired to enforce. As the boys developed, they became successful in various endeavors. She was *so* proud of them! But there was no one with whom to share her pride. Her loneliness became the hub of her depression.

After some years, Susan renewed the acquaintance of a high-school boyfriend. They dated for many months, and gradually she let down the defenses she had so laboriously erected after her divorce. She enjoyed having someone who seemed to care about her difficulties and to become excited about her successes.

But this relationship, too, failed after a couple of years. Once again the tide of loneliness threatened to engulf her. Not only did she have the present turmoil and heartache to face, but the trauma of years past began to recur in her dreams and memories.

This time, however, Susan was ready to cope. She began to pursue hobbies. Always a good gardener, she planted and tended seeds. She made herself talk with her boys and friends, kept busy reading, and deliberately chose to feel good most of the time. It occurred to Susan as we talked that she may have avoided her depression rather than lived through it. But as I observed the twinkle in her eye, heard her honesty, and sensed the inner strength that had sustained her, I knew that was not true.

Susan had discovered her own good answers to depression. She certainly admitted the pain and, even in the second event, faced the turmoil of the new loss. But in her first experience, she had, against her will, given in to the anger and helplessness. She wallowed hopelessly for many weeks before time and her basic health triumphed. Susan did not forget those hard-learned lessons, and when the familiar patterns of pain reasserted themselves, she was ready for them. She chose to do something pleasurable and productive, to talk about the indignation enough to dull its edge, and then turned her love to her sons, her friends, and herself.

Susan is a model for all lonely single parents. If you share her situation, I'm sure you hurt over the abandonment you've endured. Yes, you have desires and needs without anyone to care or offer comfort or support. But you have more resources within you than you may have realized. Dig until you discover them and put them to work for you!

Senior Citizens

Seeing my aging mother-in-law choose to enter a retirement home was one of the major inspirations of my life. She had lived alone after her husband of some fifty years died suddenly of a heart attack. A number of widowed older women lived in her small town, and they had some great times. They went to nearby towns for dinners, attended a variety of church and community events with great interest, and met in one another's homes for sewing, meals, or just good conversation.

The day inevitably came, however, when Mrs. K. could no longer maintain adequate care of her home or herself alone. After much talk and private consideration, she decided to sell the household items her children could not use and move into one room in a retirement center.

Mrs. K. sat on the front porch of her home of some thirty years, watching precious possessions, filled with memories, auctioned off for quarters and dollars. Finally, her house was empty. Her composure and dignity never wavered. She faced her change of residence with a courage I have rarely seen.

Mrs. K. set up the possessions she could keep and made her room as attractive and familiar as she could. Then she set about becoming a model for other residents. She went for walks, visited her neighbors, complimented the cooks, cajoled the other residents into joining her involvement with planned activities, sewed doll clothes on her old "Singer" for disadvantaged children, read to the blind, and listened to the lonely.

She visited her nearby children weekly and chatted on the phone. Yet, at times, when I would unexpectedly stop by for a visit, I would detect the sadness in her face and sense the depression in her voice.

I suspect Mrs. K.'s fairly mild depression was due to two factors—the loss of her familiar old home and friends, and the awareness of the unendurable depression of the many people there in the center who were totally alone.

Never before had I personally known people who had not a single living relative. I tried to imagine how immense and terrifying such loneliness must be. They had to make plans to dispose of all their belongings, plan their own funerals, and arrange for their own burials—alone.

Only the Census Bureau knows, I suspect, how many such people are in the United States. Living on the streets, in public or private institutions, or in mansions, these lonely people must end their days in despair. (We discussed this earlier in the chapter on depression in older people.)

Recently I asked a dear older friend about living alone. She is a diminutive lady who exudes wit and charm, and she has many friends. Only the faintest moisture filmed her eyes before she composed herself and shared some of her emotions.

It was primarily at night, she revealed, that loneliness would assail her. She often awoke in the middle of the night, and fears about her future would surround her like ghosts. She would worry about the possibility of becoming disabled. She was fiercely independent and wanted no one to ever have to wait on her or, heaven forbid, to pity her! What if her well-managed money would be consumed in costly care? What then?

Her answer to these nightmarish experiences is worth sharing. She makes herself awaken enough to gain control of her thoughts and feelings. She reminds herself of the decisions she has made, the people she has trusted to help her take care of all the eventualities possible, and the heavenly Father who has promised to never leave or forsake His children. She then reads for a while and soon falls back asleep. She emphatically states that her common sense and practicality enable her to stay out of depression most of the time. Nevertheless, she adds, there are times when the best of her efforts fail, and she faces the universal depression of the single senior citizen.

Depression's treatment will be described later, but in the case of loneliness, there are some suggestions for help that just can't wait.

- Become your own best friend. Look within to discover resources for enjoying life that are not dependent on others.

- Explore relationships with others. Through contacts at work, in your neighborhood, a church or synagogue, a night class or interest group, look for people who are interesting. Talk with them, share activities, and find a few friends.

- If you are lonely within your family, like Karen, seek counseling. An outside observer can help you find solutions to an unhealthy, unhappy marriage. Then, like Susan, choose to develop your own interests and practice good feelings.

- Even if you are older and alone, you can always find someone who needs you. Cultivate the habit of giving your love, time, and energy to others, and you will be amazed at the joy you find.

- Practice the skill of choosing positive thinking. "Fix your minds on the things which are holy and right and pure and beautiful and good" (Philippians 4:8 PHILLIPS). You can choose to feel good!

10

Seasonal Changes

*K*ris struggled with her Christmas shopping list. It was difficult to imagine, through the gloom of her mood, what her energetic boys would like, and when it was time to focus on her mother and sister, the task was impossible. For several weeks Kris had been aware of the annual recurrence of depression that began in November, peaked about New Year's Day, and seemed magically gone by early February. She wanted the special winter holidays to be memorable for her children, but each year she had more difficulty coping.

Hearing Kris's story reminded me of other friends and patients I had known through the years. Some years ago I worked with a young woman who had insisted that she became unexplainably depressed each autumn. From October through January she had to fight with all her willpower to get to work and keep her apartment in order. In her spare time she collapsed in extreme depression and inertia.

At the time I was convinced that her autumnal blues had developed out of the years of difficulties she had faced with school. As I questioned her, she could vividly recall hating school, feeling stupid, and believing herself to be ugly and different from her classmates. As the year wore on, I theorized, she would resign herself to her fate and get through the rest of the term by anticipating the freedom of summer.

So many therapists have discovered enough similar cases that there is a popular diagnosis known as *seasonal affective disorder* (SAD). One of the most common places to find this disorder is in Alaska. For many years, the rate of suicides in northern Alaska has been found to be disproportionately high. No one can explain this on the basis of academic, business, or social stress, for these factors are perhaps less competitive than elsewhere.

In my opinion, the best explanation may have to do with the three factors of extreme cold, many days of near-total darkness, and some degree of isolation. During the weeks when the earth tips so the North Pole is farthest away from direct sunlight, many people see no daylight at all. They see only dusk, and when there are clouds, the darkness deepens.

Researchers believe that sunlight plays a vital role in human physiology that affects the biochemistry of the brain and nervous system. In people who are especially susceptible to this influence, depression may be the result. We do not know why some people suffer more than others.

I, of course, believe it is due to the forces of family influence, the impact of the environment, and heredity and other physical factors that surround and are influenced by stress. (See the Introduction if you need to refresh your memory on these points.) Even rainy days can make people depressed if they are frustrated by the limitations the rain imposes. If, on the other hand, they can focus on the coziness of being sequestered from a storm, a dreary day can become a joy.

The facts that have become clear are very convincing. The disorder is usually limited to the winter months in climates that experience significantly less sunlight during that season. The average age of onset of the seasonal affective disorder is about twenty-seven years, and the great majority of the sufferers (86 percent) are women.

Kris is a perfect example of the effectiveness of taking control of her behavior and attitudes. Last year she prepared a plan long before her autumn "blahs" could attack. She did all the tasks she hated the most in October when the leaves had turned brilliant colors and she felt full of energy. Next she took care of her Christmas gift list and some of her shopping. She kept the celebrations of Thanksgiving Day, Christmas, and New Year's simple and yet carefully preserved the special traditions her family loved.

Next she planned a careful exercise routine. Each morning she would walk or do specific, vigorous exercises at home. Again in the evening Kris dutifully carried out her physical activities. Many days, as the end of November approached, she found herself wanting to stay in bed. But she knew what that would do to her depression, and she had decided she wanted to feel good.

Kris also determined to follow a good diet specifically for her. She included fruit and vegetables with a careful balance of proteins (meats, eggs, and cheese), carbohydrates (sugars and starches), and fats. As a nurse, she knew what a well-balanced diet should be. For the first time in her life, she managed to fix all the favorite holiday treats for her family without overindulging in them.

If you do not know what constitutes a really appropriate diet, call your doctor's office. The nurse there can probably send you a suggested one or can help you find one. If you have any problems with metabolism or digestion, it might be well worth the cost to visit a dietitian or nutritionist. Your local hospital will almost certainly have one of these specialists on the staff as will your area school district.

Besides her attention to a healthy diet, Kris decided to add a simple vitamin and mineral supplement to her daily regimes. Let me caution you about extra vitamins, however, because I know our health-conscious culture advocates what I fear may be excessive amounts. Our bodies can use only small amounts of these essential food elements, and most of them are adequately provided in the daily diet.

If you decide to supplement your diet with vitamins, do so carefully. Read the label to make sure you avoid preparations that generously offer two or more times the minimum daily requirement. In this case, do not buy the philosophy, "If a little is good, a lot will be wonderful!" Too many vitamins can damage your body. Obtain a simple minimum-daily-requirement type that is water soluble. If the label does not give this information, go to your local drugstore and ask the pharmacist. Vitamins prepared in a fat base are going to be stored in your body, making it very likely that you will accumulate too high a level in your body's tissues.

High stress levels that help cause depression and anxiety do seem to metabolize (or burn up) vitamins more rapidly than when stress levels are lower. So Kris was wise to give herself added protection.

Normally, Kris was a night person. After her family retired and the house was quiet, she could relax and do all the personal things she enjoyed. She decided during this period, however, that she would get extra rest. She regulated her bedtime as well as the rest of her life. She read in bed until she fell asleep and found, to her surprise, that she read less, slept more, and awoke feeling refreshed.

Kris also worked very hard on her attitude. Her life habit was to prepare for the worst because she could then handle anything less bad with certain ease. She discovered that preparing for negative events often kept her preoccupied with them, and she realized this pessimistic thinking could set off a mood of despair.

By January, usually her worst time of the year, Kris was feeling so well that she began to forget her special regimes. And gradually she tapered off her efforts till she reached a basic level of good living habits. Her face showed the elation she felt as she told me her success story.

The best part of all of this was, she reported, that she didn't need a single prescription or an hour of therapy. She had done it all by herself. As I have stated repeatedly, therapy and medication are not only okay, they are often mandatory. But sometimes, with careful self-evaluation, excellent self-discipline, and good common sense, you can do it on your own.

Kris did not realize the beneficial effect of bright lights on SAD victims, and it seems important that she improved so much without that help. Some people have been found to improve significantly after several periods of sitting in bright artificial light or a sunlamp. Those periods needed to be a couple of hours in length and repeated regularly, or the depression would return.

Treating SAD

From examples and research we can collect facts to use to overcome depression. If you suffer from seasonal affective disorder, here are the steps to follow to avoid it.

1. As autumn approaches, keep your house more brightly lighted than usual. Keep lights on whenever your house becomes too shaded. It will increase your electricity bill a little, but it will be much less costly than psychotherapy or despair.

2. Suffering from SAD does *not* mean that you are abnormal or that you are losing your mind. I find many deeply depressed people add to their problems the worry of impending insanity. This type of depression has no such implication.

3. Although light is essential in treating SAD, I strongly recommend Kris's plan of action: *(a)* take control of your attitudes and thoughts; *(b)* become disciplined about exercise; *(c)* control your diet, and take a minimal vitamin supplement to keep your body healthy; *(d)* get extra rest; *(e)* keep a positive mental attitude; and *(f)* let your faith work for you. When you feel down, there is a natural reminder of the need for energy beyond your own. Listen to and obey your "still small voice" reminding you to communicate with your heavenly Father.

Contagion of Depression

The lines on his sun-bronzed face were once those of smiles and laughter. His teasing eyes rarely twinkled anymore, and he seemed to retreat more and more into a world of silence to which I could not find a doorway. As a child, I had no words to describe it, but my father, the center of my world, was depressed. True enough, it was understandable. Times were economically depressed, and he was responsible for a large family.

I comprehended much of that, but as a child of four and five, I only *really* knew that my father was different. At times I believed it was my fault, but he rarely reprimanded me, and my childish play could occasionally elicit some of his old, familiar warmth and cheerfulness. I became anxious, too, over his depression and worries, and though Dad's problems were temporary, I had observed how it feels to be depressed.

You need to understand how "catching" depression is and its long-term impact on others. Even as an adult, you have no doubt experienced the effect of being around a truly depressed person. The more you try to cheer that person, the more frustrated you feel. By the time you can get away, you are likely to be seriously depressed yourself for a little while.

Imagine, then, the impact of a parent's depression on an infant or a child. If you happen to be a mildly or temporarily depressed parent, you may be tempted to deny the fact and to hobble along enduring your blues. I urge you not to give in to this temptation. You may be setting a pattern for depression in the mind and emotions of your children. And in them, it could become severe later on.

When you are emotionally down, the last thing you feel like doing is taking action. Even helping your mood to improve can seem such a monumental task that you believe it simply is not worth it. You can't do it. You'd rather stay down. Being depressed may even make those about you more considerate and even solicitous. No matter how tempting it is, do not yield! By taking action, you can climb out of that pit of despair, and you can help your children come out of their anxiety over you and resume their normal development.

Someday you will be old and are likely to need to lean on your adult children at times. You will want them to be strong and loving, able to cheer you in your declining years. If you have taught them too well how to be depressed, they will not likely be able to sustain you.

By now you know that becoming undepressed takes effort, but expending that effort is well worth your while!

11

Sexual Dysfunction

More than three decades ago, I was startled by an article in a well-known women's magazine. The writer described the increasing divorce rate and expressed concern about its impact on our culture. She explained with prophetic insight that as people experienced personal loss, insecurity, and depression from family breakdown, they would likely resort to increased sexual activity to find some sort of intimacy. I have seen her ideas demonstrated and share her concern. When people lose the frankness and trust that can build permanent, healthy family intimacy, they are driven to seek a tangible, physical relationship that can feel like real intimacy. How disappointed they are when they discover its shallowness.

I sat waiting my turn to discuss a current issue on a local television station. The lights revealed all the glamour of modern-day media settings, and the gorgeous newscaster was reporting the day's events and weather.

A gentleman sitting beside me in a well-tailored gray suit began quietly chatting about a news event that focused on certain problems of the homosexual segment of our world. "A friend of mine," he commented, "who knows a great many *gay* people says he never knew one who was truly *happy*." We agreed that it is a peephole into tragedy that a group of people, who experience immense sadness, should have come to call themselves gay.

This businessman's insights were on target. Many of the homosexuals I have known have confided that, frankly, they are miserable people. They feel one sexual identity, but their physical selves do not fit their feeling. And their bodies do not fit the homosexual acts in which they engage. They live in a strange dilemma and become, almost of necessity, defensive about their life-style. Perhaps because of this basic, unconscious depression, they have reacted in an opposite direction—trying to find in gaiety the true happiness many of them lack.

Years of research have failed to uncover any definite answers to the creation of homosexuality. According to the best recent research, it appears to be the result of very early life experiences, and that is certainly true of the patients I have worked with.

These people (my patients) have suffered extreme depression. They experience intense anger—not just about their sexual predicament, but toward their parents, authority figures in general, and themselves. They are sad about the losses and events that have repeatedly brought pain into their lives. They feel trapped and helpless and, finding no way out, believe any solutions are hopeless. They often feel profound guilt and are extremely frightened of the consequences of homosexuality. Every component of serious depression is present in these lives.

I must add that some gay people have loudly protested that the happy and healthy gays simply do not go to psychiatrists or therapists. And I certainly can see that point. However, the experiences of my friends and patients and those of contacts like my companion in the television studio convince me that few indeed are the gays who are truly *gay* (that is, lighthearted or happy).

Dr. George Rekers, a brilliant research psychologist, has been studying the factors that contribute to the creation of homosexuality. He has verified in most cases the primary dysfunction of the family as the primary cause of this sexual identity problem. He has found, as I have, at least one parent who is at best cold or distant (and has been since childhood) and another who has negative feelings about one sex.

Let me give you an example. Bill was the youngest son in a family of several children. At the time he was about two, it became apparent that his parents disliked each other. Mom would often complain of her husband's stupidity, and she made it clear that he was an incompetent, bumbling nincompoop. Furthermore, she generalized her pronouncements to include all men as being dumb or bad.

Bill was a sensitive, observant little boy, and he noticed that when Dad tried to fix a leaking sink, his efforts often resulted in a flooded kitchen and finally a call to the local plumber. Not wanting to become a bumbling idiot like his father, as his small-boy perceptions saw him, Bill spent more time with his powerful, competent mother. He learned, out of fear of her disapproval, to think, act, and feel like her.

Tragically, according to his description, Bill found himself as an adolescent strangely attracted to boys as dating companions. He was horrified that he could not feel sexually excited by girls. He did not want to be a homosexual, but those early messages, heard and responded to at such a young age, had left their mark. Bill suffered extreme anguish over his dilemma and was severely depressed for many years. Fortunately, Bill was one of the few homosexuals I personally know who was able to extricate himself from that life-style and make a happy marriage. It took years of help, strong self-discipline, and an understanding sweetheart, but he made it. Few do.

Bill taught me much of what I know about gay thinking and feeling. He described and revealed the early pain, confusion, and fear that were caused by his parents' marital discord and his father's ineptness. All too late, he discovered many wonderful qualities in his father and was able to develop a friendship with him. He recognized deep anger toward his mother and even toward himself and described this tendency as being present in all his gay friends. He experienced deep sadness and guilt. The components of depression were his emotional companions from his earliest memories.

Other homosexual patients have not been as successful as Bill at changing, though their stories are remarkably similar. I am not certain about the reasons, but I saw differences in the level of motivation to change, less belief that change was possible, more fear of the opposite sex, and a deep yearning for intimacy with the same sex. One person would awaken from a night spent in the arms of her lesbian companion, dreaming that at last her mother was holding and loving her.

Once again, I see the close relationship of grief and depression. My patient was grieved that her mother never really loved her, and her entire life was beset by chronic depression.

Sexual Dysfunction in Marriage

In my work as a family therapist, I often hear from one spouse about unfaithfulness of the other. While traditionally it has been the husband who strayed, it is also common for a wife to have an affair. Such behavior always creates pain and anger and frequently ends in divorce.

Recently I have listened to several personal friends grieve over unhappy marriages. In each of these situations, sexual problems are a major part of the difficulty. Women may be unable to respond sexually or even affectionately to their husbands. Men may have a variety of troubles in sexual adjustments. Each is likely to blame the other and believe sexual fulfillment can be found in another partner. Due to the newness and excitement of a secret affair, many do find this to be true—temporarily. In many cases, however, where divorce and remarriage take place, old patterns reemerge and maladjustment occurs all over again.

Many sexually frustrated husbands and wives become depressed. They feel their friends are experiencing romance and believe that others enjoy the intimacy they are missing.

The conflicts and tensions of erroneous, unconscious beliefs have entrapped these men and women in a physically lonely world. As parents, they may even have difficulty showing affection to their children. They feel angry, sad, vaguely guilty, and helpless—they are truly depressed.

Husbands and wives alike add to the depression by feeling rejected and even deceived. The promise of an often delightful courtship does not reach fulfillment. They may alternate in believing that he is at fault, that he is clumsy at making love—or that she is. Thus, barriers build from both sides in these troubled marriages.

Leah illustrates a marriage in which good sexual adjustment changed. She experienced a delightfully satisfying sexual life during most of the first decade of her marriage. Short weekend honeymoons were events she and her husband cherished and anticipated with excitement.

It seemed to her, however, that almost overnight this joyful part of her marriage disappeared. Her husband started focusing his attention on business or other events. He would even discuss his preoccupations during his halfhearted lovemaking. After only a few weeks of unsatisfying intimacy, Leah became alarmed. When her husband totally refused to have sex, she feared that he was having an affair, that she had become undesirable to him, that he might never want to make love again.

Through extensive counseling, Leah understood it was not her fault that her husband had become impotent. She no longer felt guilty. She learned how to sublimate her sexual drive—to turn it into creative avenues and community service. Her helplessness was cured through this means.

She discovered that many men of her husband's age go through a decline in their sexual interests as they devote too much energy to becoming successful in business. Understanding his basic insecurity enabled her to forgive his seeming loss of interest in her, so her pain and anger subsided. One by one, Leah handled the elements composing her depression and maintained her marriage because she recognized there was a problem and obtained help to solve it. So many people fail to follow her example, make false accusations, and lose otherwise sound marriages.

Abandoned Wives

I met Nell when I was en route to a large midwestern city. I was hoping for a quiet flight so I could think and do some writing, but her eyes quietly revealed to mine that she was lonely, depressed, and needed to talk.

After only a minute of chatter about our destinations and activities, Nell began to really share. My hunch had been correct. Only a few months previously, her husband of some thirty years had asked for a divorce. His affair with a young secretary had become serious, he was madly in love with her, and he had to be free to spend the few years he might have left with her.

As I looked at Nell, I saw a gracious, silver-haired, dignified woman. As we talked, I experienced her wisdom and sensed her warmth. What could possess a man to leave such a gem?

Nell's depression, grief, and loneliness created emotional pain that was raw and intense. One of the aspects of her loss that created special distress was the sudden absence of their previously joyful sex life. Even though he was having an affair, her husband had managed to maintain their sexual intimacy. Her frustration at the time we met was accentuated by the fact that he was finding a whole new vista of physical excitement in his young sweetheart while Nell was left, like useless junk, to cope with being alone.

Neither Nell's morals nor her position in life would allow her to have an affair. Though she had considered remarriage after her divorce, she had met no one who appealed to her. And so her depression lasted—she was hurt, angry, helpless, and afraid of finishing out her remaining years alone. Both Nell and I agreed that the death of her spouse would have been easier to bear than his abandonment at this time in her life.

Every example is not like Nell's, but the result—one spouse is abandoned—is the same. In some cases an older husband has often been neglected by his wife. She has refused sexual intimacy and become self-centered. In this situation, a depressed husband may find genuine comfort and happiness, missing in his marriage for years, with another, often younger, woman.

Mid-Aged Men

Reaching the age of forty is for many people a really grim event. A coworker reached that milepost about two years ahead of me. He told me how he felt on that memorable day. He looked carefully at himself as he shaved and discovered some gray hairs in his coal-black waves. He had little lines around his eyes, and the flesh under his jaws was not as firm as he felt it should be. As he allowed the truth of his birthday to come into focus in his mind, he spoke aloud to his reflection in the mirror, "Dick, you will never again be as young and as handsome as you are today!" That simple statement expresses for most men the awareness of aging.

For those fortunate few, like Dick, who have enough inner strength and spiritual resources, this startling awareness is not a tragedy. They just continue to develop the inner beauty that knows no limits. They mellow into old age with wisdom, dignity, and experience that enriches everyone who touches their lives.

But a great many men I know have not so gracefully accepted aging. They have relied on their looks, charm, wit, and money for self-esteem. The hero worship of others is food for their empty inner beings. As they face, some for the first time, the unrelenting marks of aging and discover they have no control over the progress of time, they become depressed. They find ways to alleviate their depression that are far from healthy. They try to deny their aging by redoubling efforts to regain physical fitness. They color their hair, refuse to look at their wrinkles, dress more nattily, and discover they are attractive to other women.

Men who during their depressed state find themselves sexually impotent with their wives are often amazed to discover a renewed sexual arousal over the advances of an exciting young woman. What a miraculous means such a woman offers of proving they are not, as they feared, "over the hill." How easily they convince themselves that it is not true they are aging! Their *old* wives are at fault for no longer stimulating them, and all they need to regain virility and youth is a young wife. And that is true for a while. But time actually does march on, gray hair increasingly grows out at the part (if there is one!), and wrinkles become deeper—more undeniable proof of what's happening to them. These men move on to old age with often desperate efforts to deny it and to regain that lost youth.

The defenses of denial and rationalization can work so well that people may actually believe they are young and invincible. I believe, however, that when the inevitable truth does break through to their minds, the depression that overtakes them is even more unbearable.

My theory, then, is that older men become impotent sexually due to disarranged priorities and the expenditure of energy on work and pleasure more than on loving their wives and families. As in Leah's case, it was not because of an affair that her husband lost interest in her sexually. But having lost that part of their love life, he certainly was placed in a position of vulnerability.

I hope you are not facing sexual problems in your marriage, but if you are, do seek counsel to help you correct them before you are tempted into destructive patterns of denial or boring habits of a loveless marriage.

Single Adults

Single adults are a rapidly increasing segment of our population in the United States. Elsewhere, I have quoted reports that about 4.5 million women were living alone twenty-five years ago, but today that figure is closer to 13 million. Many men are single, too. This topic is discussed in some depth in the chapter on loneliness, but I want to point out here the depression of sexual frustration in the single person.

Though much of our society today condones free sex among unrelated persons (at least until the AIDS epidemic appeared), many prefer not to become sexually involved apart from commitment in marriage. They would even be willing to make such a commitment but for various reasons cannot find a willing marriage partner. The reluctance to make a definite contract in a marriage may be due to an individual's independence, but mainly I see this reluctance stemming from early family experiences in which parents did not get along. Another factor comes from dating or a marriage relationship that has broken up in a painful manner, destroying trust in another person. Yet another reason is the pervasiveness of narcissism. Many people are so self-centered that they do not have the ability to love unselfishly, to show the empathy and compassion that are essential in a healthy marriage.

At any rate, among the millions of singles in our society there is an immeasurable population of depressed people. Seeking some closeness through physical intimacy offers some satisfaction, but not enough to provide the lasting, profound pleasure they seek. Such seeking then yields to the tantalizing idea that a new adventure or a different person may result in ultimate satisfaction. But something is always missing in these temporary, recreational, exploitive liaisons.

The missing ingredient is the inner sense of joy, trust, and love that can fill people only when depression is healed and faith is implanted. Then they have something to give, and the trust is there for receiving. When inner health is restored, a commitment can be made, and that satisfying, total intimacy can be exchanged.

Treating Sexual Depression

Homosexuality

Of all sexual dysfunctions, homosexuality is the most difficult to treat because its inception is so closely entwined with parental problems that date to a very early period in life. Furthermore, most of the influences on its formation are highly *un*conscious, both in the parents and in the child. Besides this, many groups now promote gay rights as their "cause," and by the very nature of the homosexual condition, there is a tendency to join and fight for a cause. In some way such a fight expresses the frustration and eases the hurts that surrounded those early experiences.

By the way, I am aware of the research that has tried to pinpoint a physical, genetic factor in homosexuality. Such research is not convincing to me and certainly is not as clearly explanatory as the social factors.

Many psychotherapists will not even attempt to effect a change from a homosexual to a straight life-style. It takes so long and so often results in failure that few can afford the time or risk the disappointment; most homosexuals cannot afford the money it costs to work toward the change.

The emotional components of depression are especially strong in the homosexual. The power of the controlling parent leaves an almost unbeatable, deep-rooted sense of helplessness. The child learned to counter the strong parent's control with an equal and opposite passivity. Seeming to give in, the child actually accumulated a passive form of aggression. In therapy this blocks progress since most patients transfer to the therapist the feelings and habits they had with their parents.

With excellent motivation and a therapist who can avoid power struggles and yet stay clear and honest with a patient, an individual can have hope for recovery with a carefully self-disciplined heterosexual life. Extreme care should be exercised in reviewing childhood experiences and attitudes and in finding out why parents felt and acted as they did. It is important to avoid blame and bitterness toward parents, but through information and understanding can come genuine forgiveness. Through this forgiveness the individual can become free from the pain, anger, guilt, fear, and helplessness of depression.

Many self-help groups have formed, and most of these are extremely useful. People who have struggled with a specific problem and have overcome it can understand those who suffer from a similar problem and help them in ways the very best of professionals cannot do. A group for homosexuals who want help with their identity or with their emotional distress is called Exodus. Contact with this group may not appeal to all homosexuals, but it *could* be a turning point in their lives. They should consider the possibility of changing, search for a special source for help, and not be afraid to try. There is hope.

The Frigid Woman

No matter what you were taught about sex as a child or what sort of role models your parents were, you, too, can change. Usually professional help is needed to uncover those old beliefs and replace them with healthy, accurate information. Seek help and work to find the fun and excitement the Creator intended you to enjoy. It will not be easy to explore sensitive areas of your life, and it will demand changes in habits as well as attitudes. Your success will almost certainly be achieved more readily if your husband will explore with you the answers you need.

They are difficult to find, but some excellent therapists specialize in sex therapy. These counselors have studied the complex interactions of mind, emotions, and body as they affect sexual functioning, and one of them can be invaluable to you as you work through your sexual problems.

I strongly recommend spiritual counsel from a well-informed clergy person of your faith. Many people have misperceptions involving their religion that needlessly inhibit their normal sexual drive. A good pastor can help you understand your spiritual values more accurately.

The Impotent Man

I have found that most men sincerely believe they should not need counseling. They have been taught to be strong and to work out their own difficulties. They are very likely, because of these beliefs, to resist the therapy that could restore their normal marital sex life. Help could prevent the dangerous attempts to prove themselves through affairs that cause so much heartache. And curing their impotence would also relieve the depression associated with it. Their wives would be delighted, and the parental joy would certainly create a happy climate for children.

Men, it is *not* a sign of weakness to admit you need help. It is, instead, a sure indication of a committed love, good judgment, and exceptional wisdom to face your needs and courageously seek the guidance that will help you meet those needs.

When you and those who love and need you most are endangered by your denial of a need, and they are made more secure when you are honest, how can anyone lose? I suggest for you, as for a frigid woman, a good, sensible sex therapist. Furthermore, this person should work with your physician to be certain there is no physical reason for your impotence. You, too, can recover!

Singles and Widowed Persons

The sexual problems in this group can be categorized. Let's consider the specific types of individuals concerned and how they can find answers to their problems.

1. *Those who are unable to find a person to whom they would be willing to make a marriage commitment.* My experience, and that of many other therapists, reveals that in this category are those who seriously lack self-esteem. They cannot believe anyone would really love them. Many in this group have had poor relationships with one or both parents, and it seems like too big a risk to enter into a permanent partnership.

   Therapy is extremely useful to you if you belong to this group. You can learn that information you believed as a child influenced your entire attitude and belief system. As an adult, with your adult mind and your counselor's help, you can replace that old system of beliefs with new and solid facts.

2. *Those who are too focused on themselves to be willing to risk giving.* Some of you in this category are just afraid and can be readily helped by good counseling. If you can admit to being self-centered and depressed, therapy will fairly quickly afford you relief. However, if you are unaware of feeling depressed and have convinced yourself you simply do not *need* anyone as an intimate life companion, the outlook is less positive.

   Actually self-focused, narcissistic individuals are not likely to read a book on depression. So you, the reader, may be frustrated by a loved one who fits the description. You will find yourself desperately trying to make this person more loving or warm. Beware! The truly narcissistic person is not at all likely to change. He has found a way to feel comfortable, and he is not going to lose that comfort by sharing either your pain or your joy. He is empty but does not realize it. He is unable to mourn and does not want to do so. He can feel only anger, and that makes him feel safe. He will add to your depression, not your joy, and he is not likely to change.

   If you discover that you are married to a narcissistic spouse, I strongly encourage you to seek marriage counsel. You have three choices—to leave the marriage (a choice not open to many who firmly believe in permanent commitment to marriage), to be miserable in the marriage, or to discover ways to grow in your own total being. A good therapist can help you make a wise personal choice.

3. *Those who have tried in vain to meet their needs through repeated sexual encounters.* You (or friends of yours) need to look closely at the reasons for engaging in a shallow, recreational type of sex. If you can be truly honest, I suspect you will discover that your depression is a little less severe when you engage in sexual play. Since you feel a little bit better, you try harder, believing or hoping you will feel even better. But somehow you never do.

This is called a *neurosis* or a *neurotic pattern* in living. Neuroses simply do not succeed in gaining their desired ends. I suggest you stop all sexual activity for a while and use your energy to focus on the fundamental causes of your depression. Whether those reasons are present stresses, faulty habits of thinking, feeling, and acting, or basic personality weaknesses, you can do something about them. Many people can help themselves, but insights may be most readily available through counseling. Do not postpone obtaining your answers. Life can be so rewarding, but you cannot experience this fulfillment when you are depressed. So get on with finding joy.

If you are single and depressed because of sexual frustration, there are answers. Admittedly, the solution may not be perfect. If you feel that sex apart from marriage is wrong, you will find yourself in a trap—frustration if you refrain from sex, guilt if you engage in it. Many people choose to live a life of celibacy, which involves the process of *sublimation*—the practice of using up your basic sexual energy in a creative, loving manner of life. Expend your love on people who are lonely and need your friendship. Develop job skills until they are excellent; discover and practice hobbies and find a worthwhile cause; learn to love and accept yourself. Your entire community as well as yourself can profit from this—and you will not be depressed.

12

Disability and Illness

*A*s *long as* my memory is intact, I shall not forget this scene. A circle of the most beautiful children imaginable were sitting around me. Their beauty was not physical, for each was cruelly deformed in some manner. The incongruity of their personal, spiritual loveliness, housed in such twisted bodies, made them so unforgettable.

My mission was to inform them that one of their classmates was not able to return to their special class from the hospital. He was dying. Each of these children knew in a unique way that he or she would not live a normally long life, but to face the imminent death of one of their members was a heavy blow.

As gently as I could, I revealed the seriousness of their friend's state. I found that I needed to say very little, for they intuitively understood. And they began to mingle their tears with gentle touches and comforting words. One child had lost her grandfather, and she recalled her feelings of loss from that memorable event. Another had mourned the death of his pet—a favorite cocker spaniel. As he sobbed out the remembered pain at this special loss, a tiny girl sitting near him twisted her entire body around in order to gently pat him with the motherly reassurance we all crave when we hurt.

The reactions of these remarkable children were focused on the current terminal illness of a classmate. The children were incredibly able to extend their awareness of grief to other profound losses both recent and past. I believe their capacity to cope so compassionately and appropriately with the pain of mourning lay in their having learned to accept their own extreme physical disabilities.

What I observed in them I have also discovered in many other people who have to live with the knowledge of their own untimely deaths or painful illnesses. In each case, there is an intricate interweaving of grief and depression that makes it difficult to know which is paramount. Whether the patient is young or old, all of the components of depression are likely to be present.

The emotions that are common in all depression are predictable in the lives of those who suffer protracted illnesses.

Children

The length of illness in children that is likely to be accompanied by depression is much shorter, of course, than in adults. Due to the inexperience of the young and the fear and anxiety they feel, time passes slowly. An illness of a few days or weeks will seem to a child of six at least as long as some months to an adult.

When children suffer from truly prolonged illnesses, then, such as cancer, severe heart disease, cystic fibrosis, or other inevitably fatal diseases, their reaction will certainly include depression. Sooner or later, they will discover their helplessness to get well. Their inability to enjoy daily fun or competition with friends and to anticipate long-term goals will inevitably be frustrating. Some children experience extreme anger at these limitations. Often they feel guilty about the burden their care imposes on the family. They frequently imagine that they have done something to bring such an illness upon themselves. The fear of pain, medical or surgical procedures, and separation from home and loved ones can only be imagined. And the ultimate fear of death itself becomes a daily awareness to the victims of such illnesses.

In my opinion, whether one calls such deep emotions, in total, depression or grief is not important. What does matter is the recognition and sharing of each, as it emerges, by a caring and empathetic adult. The adult must somehow find the way to enter into the child's experience with hope and optimism for such daily achievements and fun as can be found. This positive approach must always be an attempt to balance the pain and futility regarding long-term recovery—no small order!

Parents who are experiencing their own grief and anxiety will surely find this role heroically difficult. I recommend to such parents that they establish a strong support group. They will need help in giving the physical care that at times is exhausting. They will function much better overall if they will turn over the care of their child to trusted relatives or friends and take short vacations. And I am certain they will cope better if they have a wise pastor who can understand their anger at God and support their often-sagging spiritual faith.

Helping a child understand the death of a loved one is a truly difficult task. To enable a child to accept or comprehend his own inevitable death seems nearly impossible. A story I heard once offers the best model I have found for attempting this task.

A father was asked by his daughter of seven years what it would be like to die. After a moment her father replied, "Do you remember when you were little how you would fall asleep in front of the TV in the living room? I used to pick you up, carry you to your bedroom, and tuck you in bed. You didn't even wake up until in the morning. Then you'd ask, 'Daddy, how did I get here?' That's how I think it will be. You'll fall asleep here and when you wake up, your heavenly Father will be there to take care of you."

This father had been inspired to find an example his child could understand and translate into another context. You may find a different example, but if you are faced with the agonizing task of explaining inevitable death or severe loss of functioning, look for such parallels. Helping a child face untimely death or the limitations of chronic illness will stretch you as nothing else.

While the example just given conveys an important message about depression and grief in fatal illnesses, such events are limited in number. Fortunately, young people rarely suffer such severe diseases.

Far more frequently, however, young people and children are afflicted with frustrating and limiting illnesses. At the psychiatric hospital where I work, we always have several patients who suffer from diabetes. They rebel at the regimentation this disease creates for their entire existence. They must calculate and limit their calories and even exact amounts of the three food elements. Their exercise must be regular, and every day they have to take (and eventually give to themselves) one or more injections of insulin. Blood and urine tests must be done frequently in order to monitor their blood sugar level.

Having to live with these restrictions can be immensely painful, and many young people simply rebel. They neglect their diets or forget their shots. They almost always suffer severe depression and may even become suicidal.

Adults

Most adults have had to suffer with a loved one who has learned that cancer has been diagnosed in them. The very word creates fear, helplessness, and great sadness because of the likelihood of pain and an untimely death. Most cancer victims experience a period of anger that such a disaster has befallen them.

Having tried to be of support to a number of cancer victims very close to me, I realize that I have felt angry—sometimes at God, who would allow this disease. Those of us who can do so little for a person we love can also become depressed. Helplessness, sadness, anger, fear, and often guilt are present in both victim and loved ones—the inevitable components of depression.

Recently a friend visited me. She had learned that her brother, a homosexual, had been exposed to AIDS. In fact, the one with whom he was living was dying of that dreaded disease.

Unbelievable numbers of people are now infected with AIDS. Its extended course and the eventual death of its victims create incalculable suffering, personal isolation, and financial costs that are disastrous. The families of AIDS sufferers are often dealt a double blow. They discover the different life-style their loved one has chosen at the time they learn of this highly fatal disease. Their shock is often followed by depression with all of its manifestations.

Perhaps you have sat, as I have, by the silent bedside of a friend or relative who has suffered an accident or stroke that creates a coma. In many situations, this insult to the brain and nervous system leaves horribly crippling damage if the victim survives at all.

A mother is left in midlife with paralysis of her left arm and leg. A man at the peak of success in his profession learns that his keen mind no longer functions as it once did. He gropes for basic words that once flowed smoothly from his eloquent tongue. They learn they will never fully recover. They and their families and friends are going to have to cope with depression.

I could list a textbook full of painful, frustrating, and incurable physical illnesses that are severely complicated by depression. Multiple sclerosis, ALS (amyotrophic lateral sclerosis), and a host of neurological diagnoses that progress slowly but relentlessly leave their victims weaker and more dependent every month. They understand sooner or later that nothing can stop the course of their trouble. Cystic fibrosis, certain types of heart disease, blindness or deafness, as well as a variety of deformities, are present as birth defects that must be dealt with for life. Mental retardation with its limitations is also usually present at birth, though it may result from severe illnesses or accidents.

How Others Have Coped

As depressing as it is to write about such conditions, those who must live and cope with them have immeasurably more depression! I have been blessed, however, as I have learned from the silent, unsung heroes who have discovered how to cope successfully. Here are some of their secrets that can help you.

1. At first they denied the facts about the diagnosis. Many traveled to far away places and spent much money in search of evidence that their doctor was mistaken.

2. Eventually they faced the truth about the illness. They stopped the frantic search for some other opinion, though the original search was useful to them in final acceptance.

3. They endured and completed the grief process. Facing serious, limiting illnesses includes a loss and often multiple losses. They have resigned themselves to their lot after going through the denial, anger, and blame that are almost universal.

4. They have formed a plan or philosophy to live by. This plan includes a positive mental attitude, physical care, and resources for all kinds of help.

5. They have developed a support system composed of a variety of helping people and resources to meet medical, legal, financial, social, spiritual, and personal needs. They are not afraid to call on those resources and do not feel guilty (very often!) because they have needs.

6. Most of them cultivated their spiritual strength and openly practice their faith in a practical manner.

7. Each of them resolved to make of every day the most enjoyable and productive one possible.

8. They specifically sought support from others with a similar condition. Knowing how another coped with a problem like their own was both enlightening and reassuring.

Most people who suffer from chronic diseases overcome their fear and depression remarkably successfully. It is their relatives and close friends who seem to have the greater difficulty.

As often as possible, I dropped by to see Jackie (not her name) who was terminally ill with cancer. I intended to cheer her and relieve the boredom of her confinement. She had been ill over a year, and none of the medical treatments had slowed the relentless progress of her disease. We both silently knew her death was not far away.

My helplessness became infuriating. I could not fight the pain for her nor stop its devastation. I could offer no hope for getting better tomorrow or next week. I hated the separation death would soon put between us.

Jackie was the one who often cheered me. She found a certain challenge in facing and transcending her pain. It was a relief when her pain medication took effect permitting welcome easement. Her faith brought the strength of God into her experience, and she had come to anticipate the day her spirit would finally be released from her weakening body. And yet, she reassured me, my visits were comforting and made the day more bearable.

If you must stand by and see your loved one suffer, you are almost certain to feel angry, frustrated, and helpless. These feelings are normal, even though they hurt. And you (as does your suffering friend) need to resign yourself, accept that helplessness, and then go on to whatever you can do to help.

How to Help

Whatever the cause of another's depression, there are some responses you need to know and some actions you may need to take. Some of these are listed elsewhere, but they bear reinforcing.

1. In case of mild depression, listen with a caring heart to the feelings and problems and try to help the victim discover both the cause and solution. Help him recall the day it began and what happened at that time so he can come to a decision regarding it.

2. Offer frequent reminders of the power to choose. In the mind of a depressed person, it will seem he has no such choice. Your

job is to help him discover at least some small element of good decision making and help him put it into effect.

3. Empathize, don't sympathize. This may seem an unfair line of distinction. But by this I mean, try to put yourself in the other's place and understand something of how he feels. To sympathize or pity is to reinforce the helpless, negative aspects and makes one feel even worse.

4. Avoid minimizing the other's problem. A well-meant phrase to reduce a big problem is, "You're making a mountain out of a molehill!" Such may be the case, but a person who is reduced to peering over a molehill truly sees it as a mountain. That person needs a response to *her* feelings and perceptions, not *yours*.

5. Help the depressed person focus on individual emotions. When he can understand his anger, recognize his hurt and fear, and release his guilt, he will be able to take action and hence will not feel helpless.

6. In more severe depression, the sufferer may need professional help. You may be the one to help her recognize and accept her need. Do so without a hint of any put-downs that would reinforce her fear of weakness or worthlessness.

7. Consider depression as you would a physical illness in order to avoid the once-common sense of shame about emotional illness. Any hint of such a concept is likely to add to the negative feelings of a depressed person and may make it harder to get the help he needs.

8. Remember the physical aspects of depression. Elijah in the biblical story (related in 1 Kings 19) suffered extreme depression after an unusual victory. It is certain he was fatigued, because after sleeping and eating he recovered. Help your friend get in good physical condition and it will help, if not cure, his depression.

9. Do small nurturing things for your friend. Nurture means general taking care of, not just feeding. When one is down, a small act of kindness can remind her she is loved and valued.

10. Balance listening, care, and nurture with constant directives to look for and use the person's assets. During depression, she does not feel strong and may doubt her abilities. Recount those as you observe them and suggest her putting them to work for herself.

11. In severe depression, look for signs of suicidal intent. These signs can be categorized.

   - *Physical* signs include major prolonged changes in eating, sleeping, and exercise habits.

   - *Emotional* signs include unusual irritability and anger, prolonged moodiness with refusal to talk, and extensive weeping. Any positive emotions have a fake or put-on quality about them.

   - *Social* life changes usually involve withdrawing from others. There is no desire to make or take phone calls, to go to any social event or make personal contact. Sometimes the conversations that do occur are morose and sad.

   - The *work* of the patient suffers. He can't keep up, has difficulty finishing a task, and often cannot concentrate or remember.

   - There is *no hope* in the future. This sign is evidenced by giving away prized possessions, stopping any future plans, and refusing to take health precautions. This is a serious sign of suicidal planning.

   - Personal *hygiene* deteriorates. The person who does not plan to live long or who finds life unbearable is not likely to bathe or keep her hair styled.

If you see several of these evidences in a friend or relative, insist he gets help from a good therapist.

12. Avoid promising secrecy if you have any doubt about a friend's safety. Confidences should not be betrayed *unless* they involve plans to hurt oneself or another person. Then, be sure to seek any and all resources possible to help. A close friend went through a time in which she felt she could not endure life any more. Against her wishes, I was able to get her in a hospital, and later she became extremely grateful.

If you are to help a depressed person—whatever the cause—you cannot do so alone. Work with the person, her friends, family, and therapist to establish a warm shelter of protection, care, and encouragement.

$\boxed{13}$

Religion

Recent books, articles, and lectures in fundamentalist religious circles have uniformly warned against psychological and psychiatric services. They have been described as tools of Satan with which faith would be destroyed.

A personal example will demonstrate the unfortunate polarity that has developed between mental health counselors and a certain segment of the church. I had been asked to deliver a series of seminars on family problems for a particular Protestant denomination. The seminars were part of a larger program involving evangelistic services each evening.

The sessions I held were well attended, and I felt the deep concerns of loving parents and pastors as they questioned and probed the depths of their problems. I was aware of the spiritual background of the group, so I felt free to incorporate the timeless values of the Judeo-Christian faith as I tried to help them formulate answers.

To my surprise, in the evening service the minister spoke out against the evils of psychology. Since I had heard and read such sentiments many times, I knew he meant nothing against me personally. But I was acutely aware of the embarrassment of many people around me. They physically squirmed during that service and could hardly wait to offer their apologies to me for this truly fine man's comments.

That evening I did some profound thinking about the dilemma the minister had brought into focus. I, too, am aware of the few serious risks in bad psychology. (I have discussed these in the chapter on professional treatment.) But I have seen good psychotherapy help people whose faith alone could not suffice.

As I meditated, I was reminded of an unforgettable sermon preached by a noted clergyman from Uganda, Africa. The Reverend Festo Kivengere described the miraculous event of Jesus' raising Lazarus from the dead. The point of his message was this: Christ's power certainly restored life to the dead man, but in His inimitable style Jesus included other people on His divine team. He asked those who had approached the tomb with Him to roll away the huge stone that sealed the entrance to it. Then as Lazarus responded to His resurrection call, Jesus asked them to remove the fabric that was wound about his body so he could be really free to live again.

Good mental health counselors are good team members. We can only serve as channels for the healing, revitalizing power of the Source far beyond our own. And Christ made it clear throughout His earthly ministry that such is His plan—to love and heal hurting and spiritually dead people through His disciples. All truth and health, I am convinced, come from God, but He looks for those who will serve as conduits for His qualities of good to those who have not yet discovered them.

I shared these insights with those who attended my morning seminar. Obviously, someone had revealed to the minister his unwitting put-downs of the previous evening, because he came to the session. At the close, he graciously, publicly apologized—certainly an unnecessary act. It served, however, to convince me that if people will listen to one another with open minds, and even more open hearts, many disagreements can be resolved.

Having been raised in an unusually devout family, I, too, once believed that simply turning over our lives to the heavenly Father would end life's problems and create an instantly perfect solution to them. Through profound struggles with real people in real-life situations, however, I realize this is not the entire picture.

People have blockades in their lives—mistaken information, inconsistencies in their training, and confusion in their feelings. They lack trust and often have poor judgment with which to make wise decisions. These weaknesses in the habit patterns of their lives are like the grave cloths that wrapped the body of Lazarus, limiting his vision as well as his movements.

Instead of fighting against the mental health profession, then, the church would do well to embrace it, offer time-proven values and wisdom, and learn how to more effectively minister to the broken lives of people.

In both extremes—fundamentalism and liberalism—of present-day religion you need to understand inherent values and dangers. I have had exceptional opportunities to share in depth with friends of Catholic, Jewish, and Protestant faiths. I have been involved with Pentecostals, Charismatics, and the range of fundamentalist to liberal-thinking Christians. Each group has much to offer in faith, intellectual understanding, and the practical application of values and beliefs, but each group faces certain challenges as well.

For depressed persons, each extreme poses some problems. First, let's consider the fundamentalist position and its sometimes simplistic teachings.

Fundamentalists

The denomination in which I grew up was and is one of a fervent faith in a powerful God. The leaders believed that individuals must maintain a perfect life pattern, and the church manual contained many pages of rules. Most of these rules, as I recall them, were lists of activities *not* to do. There was little mention of the joy and peace that faith can bring, and I knew little of spiritual freedom. I recall immense guilt for even small infractions of those rules and a deep fear of eternal punishment. My family offered a healthy balance through laughter, fun, and the richness of love and support, but I know that many of my church friends did not enjoy similar benefits.

A dear friend of mine grew up a devout Catholic. She married early to escape an unbearable family situation, but she made a poor choice. Her new husband was abusive, and she could not tolerate her pain. Rejected by her parents, Tammy turned to her parish priest for help. Of course, he could not condone separation, and though he truly cared about her plight, he could offer her only one recourse. "Take this rosary," he told her, "and pray your prayers daily."

Despairing of any satisfying help, Tammy took the rosary and left the church. At the nearest corner she angrily threw it into the gutter. Turning her back on her faith and her church, she entered a life of prostitution where, for years, she buried her depression beneath her cold exploitation of men whom she saw as cruel and uncaring.

In their beneficent intention to prescribe a good (even perfect) Christian life, fundamentalists may unwittingly intensify depression. A truly conscientious person is likely to strive for perfection, only to discover, with increasing guilt, fear, and helplessness, that it is impossible to achieve.

Furthermore, I have discovered that we unconsciously feel about God much as we did about our parents. Our faith, therefore, is often limited by the experiences that molded our trust (or lack of it) in our parents. Let me give you some examples.

One of my favorite pastimes as a child was to accompany my father as he worked around our farm. Nearly always Dad would ask me to wait to descend from the wagon or tractor until he reached the ground. Then with the inimitable twinkle I loved so well in his brown eyes, he would say, "Now, jump to me, Gracie!" And jump I instantly would do. I knew no fear, for Daddy's arms were strong. He never let me fall. It was easy for me to trust the heavenly Father.

But even a strong and loving father has human weaknesses. As an adult, I joined a small group to learn more about conversational prayer. One of the group gently confronted me one evening and asked why I rarely asked God for anything for myself. I had been totally unaware of this fact, but I realized my friend was right. She informed me that God really wants to give good gifts to His children and suggested I might be depriving myself of His benefits by failing to ask.

That evening I experienced a life-changing insight. As I drove home, I recalled a time during the economic depression of the 1930s. I had begged my father for some things I needed. Again and again, I reminded him of my need, and finally he provided those things. Later, I learned he had to borrow the few dollars those purchases required. I knew how much my father hated to borrow money, and I understood that I had caused him some difficulty. I remembered that I vowed never again to ask my dad for anything I did not absolutely have to have.

I realized that I had unconsciously transferred to my heavenly Father that silent, childish vow to spare my earthly father needless pain. My head knew better, of course! The God I knew was infinitely rich—yet in some degree I had limited His giving by my failure to ask and receive those gifts.

If fundamentalist churches could grasp the broad meaning of this concept, they would improve their ministries. Instead of demanding human perfection in order to please God, they should teach His unconditional love. They would help one another become channels of healing, redemption, and grace.

Instead of loading condemnation and guilt on depressed people for failing to trust God and be happy all the time, the churches would extend compassion for the pain, forgiveness for the sins, and the support suffering individuals need. Through teaching and healthy examples they would enable people to grow.

Being born again is simply not enough. Even being filled with the Spirit, as the Charismatics teach, is not enough. In a sense, the church must reparent its members. Those who have lived without a trusted dad need to learn about a totally trustworthy heavenly Father. Those who have grown up in permissive homes, without consistent training and discipline, need the benefit of loving correction from the church. They must be taught the age-old wisdom of that handbook of the Judeo-Christian world, the Bible.

The teamwork that could be established between the church

and sound mental health professionals could accomplish more than anyone dreams. The work of good therapists would be enhanced if their patients belonged to a loving, guiding, steadying support group—the church. And I know the church would be enriched as its members learned to overcome anger and pain, to give up their helplessness and sadness, and to accept forgiveness and become free of guilt and fear.

Liberals

The opposite religious extreme is equally likely to create and add to problems of depressed people. Fundamentalists are at risk for producing depression through legalistic, rigid demands and condemnation for failure to measure up. Liberals do not fall into this trap. In fact, they join mistaken mental health professionals in lowering standards and making excuses. In many cases, they have drained faith of its power. They teach, at best, a "nice" philosophy.

When people stressed and depressed by the conflicts and demands of life turn to a liberal church, they may be left without help. If God is dead and only the Book of His teachings is left, they may be worse off than with no religion. Reading of His magnificent miracles in the Old and New Testaments could stir up some exciting hopes. A God who could free His people from slavery by miraculously separating the waters of the Red Sea was a mighty force with whom Pharaoh had to reckon. But those whose minds cannot conceive of these miracles (having never seen any) deny that they ever happened. They assert that the miracles are only symbols, fables, or myths. In denying the infinite power of God, it seems to me, any real hope for help is snatched away. In my opinion, the depressed, burdened people who attend liberal churches continue because, in spite of it all, they sense the glimpses of true power. They deserve more!

As I have come to understand Him, God is a gentle being. At the dawn of creation He gave to His first human beings the power of choice. I cannot fathom His wisdom and courage in maintaining His refusal to take back that gift! Even when we, His creatures, deny

His existence and power, refuse His gifts, and reject His Spirit's wisdom and guidance into truth, He will not remove that power. I'm very sad that an apparently growing number of religious groups choose to go it alone. "Let me do it myself!" has become a spiritual concept today. People do not like to admit their weakness and need because that admission reveals their vulnerability and opens them to failure, hurts, and depression.

There Is Hope

From areas outside the organized church, perhaps there is emerging a new and sound sort of spiritual insight. Only recently a friend who had relegated God, if He did exist, to some remote sphere came to a new awareness of Him. She had joined one of the self-help groups that recognize people need a Power higher than themselves. She listened to the stories of others who had discovered God's availability and intervention for them when they finally asked His help. In a moment of desperation (that is often the turning point in a person's life), she asked Him to show her how to understand her life and what choice she should make.

According to her, answers she had sought for years began to formulate in her mind. She experienced compassion and understanding that were new to her, and she felt the courage to take action and make decisions that she had never before been able to do. Best of all, she recognized this power beyond herself for who He actually was—the heavenly Father who had been waiting all the time for her to turn to Him.

This woman has been depressed in a greater or lesser degree for most of her life. Her church did not convey to her the hope of divine help, and she had managed to hobble unhappily along on her limited resources until the stresses became too great. Then, through an unexpected avenue came her revelation. Gratefully, she responded.

Many years ago I read a condensed version of a book I can no longer find. Nor do I recall its author. He related life stories of three young men—an American Indian, a Jew, and a Catholic. Each was trained and raised in his own traditions and religious practices, which were the core of the parents' lives. But each became intrigued with exploring intellectual and material pursuits. Each neglected his spiritual life, which became dormant.

Through a series of unique stresses and extremely difficult events, each was finally driven to rediscover those early values. Each of them came to a spiritual reawakening and found the resources that restored the wholeness and balance they had lost.

I urge upon you a similar search and rediscovery. Most of us must reach our own limits before we either find our spiritual Source or use it well. You may be depressed *because* of your rigid, legalistic religious teachings and your awareness that you simply cannot measure up. God, though you really believe in Him, may seem unreachable and unavailable to you. You may even be angry with God because He seems to have abandoned you when you need Him.

On the other hand, you may have turned to a church for help with your depression and found that church had no Power to offer you. In your search for a strength greater than your own, you are chasing elusive glimpses of truth.

Let me share a very personal experience that may open up brand-new insights. I, too, have experienced times of depression (as I mentioned earlier), and I have searched for the answers to stress and my inadequacies to cope. And I have found the answers for myself that I am trying to clarify and share with you so that you may know recovery and healing for depression.

At a crucial time in my life, I had reached my limits. I had prayed earnestly, and I had faced my anger toward the heavenly Father who seemed to have abandoned me. I felt sad, lonely, afraid, and hopeless. It seemed to me I had tried everything. I had attempted to live up to those pages of rules from my childhood, but my prayers went unanswered. I might, after all, never be good enough to be accepted by God as His child.

One cold winter evening, I sat in my study meditating. I closed my eyes to shut out my environment and planned to repeat my prayers. God, however, was finally ready to speak to me—or, more likely, I was at last ready to listen to Him. I found my mind focusing on a visual image of an electrical outlet. It was, in fact, the outlet in my study, and beside it stood a lovely floor lamp. That lamp was dark, and the electrical socket was empty.

My college physics had taught me of the vast power of electricity. I knew within that outlet was enough energy to shock me or warm the room or light the dark lamp. The will and the action were needed to plug in the lamp to the power source. Suddenly I understood my dilemma. I had been trying so hard to be good and to do well because I loved God and wanted to please Him; but I had been doing most of that in my own strength. No wonder my vitality was at a low ebb and my hope nearly gone!

I knew my physics well enough to understand another spiritual insight. The power did not jump across the extension cord to the light bulb. It traveled through the fine copper wires setting every atom to dancing with energy before it reached the fine filament that created light in my room.

A lifetime of spiritual struggles was transformed for me that evening. I was not helpless. I could choose to plug in to the Power Source. Through the light that action created, I began to understand my pain and found healing as I learned to forgive. Without the pain, I no longer needed the protection of my anger, so it began to subside. My sadness dissipated as I replaced it with the joy of my discovery. The light revealed the falseness of much of my guilt and taught me to forgive and accept forgiveness for my real guilt. With such power, who could be afraid?

I learned in a variety of ways how to cope with and overcome my depression. This spiritual experience with its new insights became something like the capstone in an arch. It was the key piece that completed the work begun with therapy and continued through thinking, reading, and discussing with others the problems and issues of my life. I hate to contemplate what might have happened if I had stopped my search. The solutions have been so rewarding.

In your spiritual search I hope you find and follow these steps:

• Know there is a Power beyond your own.

- Be certain that Power is loving, creative, and positive and that He wants to be found by you.

- Remember, God will wait for you to become still enough to hear His voice and follow it to Himself.

- You will probably come to the very end of your resources before you fully accept that you need Him.

- When you establish contact with God, you are likely to be surprised by the joy He brings.

- It is essential that you recognize the need for commitment. Staying plugged in to the true Power Source is the only way that energy can consistently flow and accomplish its unique purpose.

I trust you will find, in the expression best suited to you, that unique combination of human support and help and the divine power and protection that will totally deliver you from depression!

14

Grief

In discussing depression in infants, preschoolers, and young children I attempted to clarify that what looks like depression is really grief. I gave examples of the loss of a parent through divorce and the loss of friends and playmates who moved. You, as adults, must learn to distinguish grief from depression. Grief is a strong emotional response to a loss while depression is a more vaguely expressed, though equally painful condition unrelated to any known cause.

A young father found himself unable to enjoy life, felt strangely anxious, and had difficulty sleeping. His exercises that usually relieved the stress in his life no longer had any effect. He believed he was depressed, and he had all the signs of depression.

As I have described elsewhere, however, he was not depressed. He was simply grieving over the loss of his freedom. The birth of his first child had drastically remodeled his entire life-style. The very depth of his love for his child enhanced his grief and disguised it by making him feel guilty for resenting his loss. He believed there was something wrong with him because he felt resentful, even angry, about the situation.

One counseling session with this exceptionally honest young father enabled him to recognize the classic stages of grief—denial, anger, guilt, blame, preoccupation, sadness, hopelessness, then resignation, and finally healing. Understanding that his grief was normal and seeing its components so neatly defined helped him face the task of overcoming it. Once he had experienced the healing phase, this father could truly enjoy his child and his own new role.

The voice on the other end of my phone hesitated and then stopped. I was aware of the caller's intense emotion and suspected she was silently weeping. Finally, in a voice flattened by her efforts to control herself, she told me of her severe depression and begged to see me.

Knowing well the trauma of such pain and the relief of any comfort, I arranged to see her late that evening. Doris was a dignified older woman. Her appearance was elegant, but her eyes were red with weeping. My tissue box soon registered empty as she continued to cry.

Doris told her story clearly and quickly. She and her husband had been married fifty years and had enjoyed an unusually satisfying life. Their daughters had married well, they had a good retirement, and they enjoyed their grandchildren. Only recently had her husband begun to deteriorate physically, and she could no longer take care of him at home. It was necessary for him to go to a nursing home.

Gone were her dreams of a delightful retirement with travel, leisurely mornings, evening walks, and the joy of sharing together the achievements of their grandchildren. Doris was not depressed; she was obviously grieving.

I urged her to allow herself to feel the pain, to accept her anger at the sudden loss of her dreams, and to resign herself to the inevitability of her situation. Doris was even honest enough to admit she was angry with God for snatching away her plans and hopes. For only a few more weeks I visited at intervals with this woman. She was amazed at the healing of her grief. There were many things she could not do for her husband, but she faithfully performed whatever loving deeds she could manage. Accepting the limits over which she had no control brought her through the resignation stage of grief quite soon, and she could get on with the enjoyment she could find—alone and with her friends. She even began to understand that God gives no guarantees about life's being easy—only the promise of resources for survival and healing.

All of us are aware of the major losses—of youth, health, money, friends, status, even life itself. The pain over these losses is clear and understandable. Other losses, however, are not so well defined. Victims may not connect their responses to them, and they may believe they are depressed. Let me start with early childhood and discuss some of the subtle losses that often go unrecognized.

Loss of Dependency

At about two or three years of age most children begin to experience loss. They lose the bottle and often the pacifier. They lose the comfort of their diapers and a parent's care of their toilet needs and have to learn to use the potty. They have to feed themselves, entertain themselves, and even go to bed alone. Many are having to give up parents to a younger baby. It's really no wonder children go through those "terrible twos." What a loss of dependency, attention, and ease!

Today many children must lose the familiarity and security of their own homes for the noisy confusion of day care and preschool. And many face the loss of one parent from divorce or abandonment. By the age of three, children seem to handle these adjustments better, especially if those first few years have been reasonably secure.

Loss of Freedom

At least by age five, children must face another big loss. This time they give up their dependency and freedom in a new way. They must adapt to many other children in a strange, new, regimented setting. They must attend school. Never again will they be as carefree as they have been. The real world invades their lives, and they must learn many academic and personal skills.

Most children used to cry when they started kindergarten. I believe those tears were shed for the loss of their freedom and the grief that accompanied that loss. Since so many children are now accustomed to preschools, I suspect there is less of that grief.

With the arrival of first grade, most children who have been used to only half days of school will suffer more pangs of loss of the last vestiges of early childhood freedom. I vividly remember how our youngest child felt after her first full day in first grade. As we sat around the evening dinner table, she rested her little blonde head on a chubby hand and wearily said, "Please be nice to me, Mommy! I've had a hard day!" I will always be grateful she could recognize the hardness of that day and ask for comfort. Many youngsters have not learned that recognition and seem to lack the words for asking. Such children are likely to collect their griefs and become depressed.

Ends of Eras

I believe children go through minigrief experiences at the end of each school year. If they are fortunate enough to have teachers they like and respect, this grief can be fairly heavy, though it rarely lasts very long. I've observed that the rooms of those special teachers have streams of visitors every autumn when school resumes. Frankly, I see the practice of returning for visits as a useful one. It must be a high compliment to dedicated teachers, and I know it is comforting to the children to know they are not forgotten.

Losses in Competition

Throughout the school years there are a series of contests and competitions. The value in these experiences lies in the motivation they provide for students to try to excel. The pain lies in the inevitability of someone's losing. These losses will result in grief and offer to parents and teachers the opportunity to teach children how to accept losing with poise and how to take risks by trying again. Teaching children how to recognize and work out those stages of grief is a matchless opportunity. When children know how to cope with grief, I am confident they are not likely to become seriously depressed.

Separations and Death

The loss of relationships through the moves of friends' families or the death of relatives is a major loss to many children. Recently, my nine-year-old grandson faced coping with the death of his paternal grandfather. The man had been ill for some weeks, so his death was not a great surprise. In fact, Andy told me that he knew his grandfather was sick. But Andy realized he was *really* sick when Aunt Diane came home from the West Coast.

When his mother told him about his grandpa's death, Andy cried, and then he said, "Mommy, let's not talk about it anymore. I don't want to feel this bad!" He experienced immediately the universal instinct to deny the *pain* of his loss. During the following days I watched his remarkable courage in the midst of the pain; the dignity with which he went through the service was an inspiration. He was concerned with his grandmother, and in the gentle way of a child, he tried to comfort her. He has been able to survive this first big loss of his life with strength due to the adults around him. They listened to him, shared their grief with him, and offered him comfort in the midst of his trauma.

Loss of Possessions

At last they were gone! The family who had visited Arlene and her parents had enjoyed a delightful evening. But the children had been wildly aggressive and destroyed two of Arlene's Barbie dolls. She was a careful "mother" to her dolls, tucked them in bed every evening, and generally took excellent care of them. In entertaining her guests she had been caught in a dreadful spot. She did not want to hurt their feelings, but she was horrified at their roughness. Long after their departure Arlene grieved over the destruction of her toys.

Her parents were tempted to immediately replace the dolls, knowing that it was not their daughter's fault they had been broken. But they realized she had assigned to her "babies," over the months she had them, personal traits that made them precious to her. So they listened to her anger, comforted her sadness, and helped her through the grief. Then they could replace the dolls and plan to protect them from the next onslaught of rough playmates.

A few years ago I was busily finishing my writing before the publisher's deadline. I was surprised to have a phone call in the office where I was sequestered to avoid just such interruptions. On the other end of the line was my husband's voice quoting, "Do not lay up for yourselves treasures on earth, where moth and rust destroy and where thieves break in and steal." In my instant denial, I laughed, thinking he was making a strange joke to lighten my labors.

But it was no joke! Our house had been broken into, and thieves had actually stolen our most treasured objects. They didn't bother to take appliances and furniture, but they selected my few most sentimental pieces of jewelry, each symbolic of a special anniversary in my life. They grabbed objects that had been carefully chosen as mementos of the really nice vacation trips we had taken as a family. They took our teenager's special memory box with her childhood treasures—the medals she had labored to win in track and citizenship. Gone were the gold cross and chain we had given her to commemorate her confirmation and the dainty silver bracelet from her first boyfriend.

When I saw my home ruthlessly ransacked, invaded by persons who had no right to be there much less to take our precious mementos, I knew rage. That rage was prompted by the pain of such senseless, unjust behavior and by my helplessness to do anything about it. My cherished possessions were only part of my loss. I also lost my sense of safety. My home had been my citadel—the place where I could return from the weariness and frustration of working in a troubled world. Suddenly, I knew that place of security no longer existed. It was only a house, entirely vulnerable to common robbers!

But my grief, like Arlene's, has healed, and I have rebuilt some of the sense of safety I once enjoyed. The losses of life bring grief, but knowing how to grieve ensures recovery. You need not become depressed because of such losses.

Loss of Heroes and Dreams

I grew up in an era of heroes. Charles Lindbergh crossed the Atlantic Ocean in a tiny airplane—the first time it had been accomplished! Arthur Hertzler, the horse-and-buggy doctor of the early days in Kansas, dared to surgically remove the disfiguring goiters that plagued so many women. Amelia Earhart lost her life in the Pacific. Admiral Byrd risked his life and the lives of his men to explore Antarctica. These were people who lived while I was living. I only read about Marie Curie, Elizabeth Blackwell, Abraham Lincoln, and Teddy Roosevelt. I learned to revere these heroes and struggled to copy, even remotely, their courage and achievements.

I was a natural subject for further idealization of people. Being raised in a strongly religious family, I was especially taught to respect the clergy. One clergyman I admired evidenced theological soundness, a brilliant mind, and an artistic, sensitive temperament rarely found together. Through various circumstances I came to know this man very well, and my respect for him grew.

But a dreadful rumor began that this man of God had become morally bankrupt. He was reportedly having an affair. Despite my efforts to deny these ugly bits of gossip, I discovered that they were true. He finally left his family and his ministry and married the "other woman." I had lost an ideal—a hero.

For years I was stuck in the anger stage of my grieving over this loss. Inwardly, I railed at him, and I refused to communicate with him. I had been wrong in my evaluation of him, and I was helpless to change him or his decision and actions.

After a period of years, however, enough information began to seep through my mind to my heart to enable me to understand him. Finally, it was possible to forgive him. The sad truth is, however, that he will never again be the ideal clergyman I thought him to be—I had lost an ideal person.

The pastel colors of spring flowers filled the church. Candle glow softly accented the fading light of sunset as Marsha approached the altar where Ned eagerly waited to make her his wife. The wedding was the climax of an engagement filled with dreams. She would work to put Ned through medical school. He would become a physician who would save the lives and restore the health of many people. And just as she loved him today, sometime she would be so proud of him.

But Ned found studying to be boring and the limited income, unbearable. Before long, he quit school, leaving Marsha feeling betrayed. What had become of her dreams? Somehow she had to make them come true, so she encouraged, cajoled, threatened, and even nagged her husband. It was no use. Her wonderful dreams were lost.

Marsha denied the facts as long as she could. Then she became very angry. Finally she resigned herself, recovered from her disappointment, and moved on to another dream over which she had some control. She would gain an education that would enable her to help people in her own way. A lost dream is very sad, but after the grief, new and more realistic goals can be found.

Grief and depression feel identical. Anger, sadness, helplessness, guilt, and fear are ingredients of both. And when losses go unrecognized, grief is not completed, and depression may well result. But true depression may creep up so gradually, or it may descend so rapidly, without a known reason, that its victim is powerless to understand or cope with it. By contrast, grief that is the aftermath of a loss is focused, its cause may be understood, and its relief is usually a matter of time with its healing.

If you are acquainted with grief and its stages, I predict you will be less vulnerable to depression. Of course, you must be willing to work your way through those phases with all their pain and then accept the healing process. Do not let your loyalty *or* your self-pity push you into the lengthy detours of grief that can lead to depression.

15

Fringe Benefits

In my work as an administrator, I often have the opportunity to hire new people to work in our hospital. One of the most important questions to be considered is that of the salary, and then the prospects ask, "And what are the fringe benefits?" They want to know about the health insurance, retirement program, sick leave, vacation time, and other rewards for their good work.

Having worked with depressed people for years and having experienced it myself, I have learned a great deal about depression. The basic pay for being depressed is obviously negative—it includes all sorts of bad feelings that no one wants to endure. But fringe benefits not included in that bad payoff unconsciously may keep individuals mired in a state of chronic depression.

Attention from Others

Her shoulders slumped, her head drooped, and her hands spread out in a gesture of helplessness. When her face was visible, its lines portrayed the hopelessness of her sad life. Wilma was sloppily dressed, and her hair was poorly groomed.

In a monotone that was difficult to hear, this woman began to reveal her situation. Once she had been the strength of her family. She was the encourager, the nurturing, loving, protective one for her three children and her husband. The children were now in their late teens and were busy about their own activities. Her husband had progressed to a level of responsibility in his job that consumed most of his energy and left little time for her.

Over several months Wilma had been increasingly "blue." It seemed useless to get up in the morning because the girls ate little breakfast and preferred fixing their own meal. Her husband usually had breakfast meetings and left early. When she did get up to talk with her children, they were in a hurry to leave. No one, it seemed, cared about her, and no one needed her. She was clearly depressed.

Seeking psychiatric help in her case was wise because she needed medication. Her depression had robbed her of sleep, and her poor appetite had caused a serious weight loss. I referred her to a therapist who worked with adults, but I continued to see her at times for many months. In spite of excellent medical supervision and good psychotherapy, Wilma continued to feel depressed, and she looked terrible.

One day I decided to take a risk. I said, "Wilma, it seems to me there are some fringe benefits you're receiving from staying depressed. What do you think?"

Just as I expected, she became furious. "What do you mean! I am suffering horribly! How can you think I'm getting any benefits out of this? You doctors just aren't helping me one bit!"

At once I knew I had hit the target. As Wilma exploded for several minutes, I knew she was finally giving vent to some of her stored-up anger. She turned her rage from the doctors to her ungrateful children and neglectful husband and finally reached the end of her tirade.

At last I could ask, "And how do your family members treat you since you have been so depressed?"

The change in her facial expression gave me the answer. She

grinned for the first time and remarked, "They've been so kind and considerate. They try to talk to me at times. I almost feel like I'm important to them once more! I think I see now what you mean."

The severity of their mother's depression awoke her daughters to her need of them, and they had begun to pay attention to her. That too-busy husband had to face his unwitting neglect and began to notice his wife. He began to touch her more and tried to help bring her back to the happiness she had once expressed.

But Wilma was not to be fooled by the efforts of her family. She knew how far away from her they had grown, and her common sense said, "If you get well, they'll all go right back to ignoring you again. So stay a little bit sick and keep them close to you."

Self-Pity

Self-pity may also somehow make depressed persons feel better. Private sufferers may give themselves some special attention that otherwise they would feel guilty about. They may spend money they cannot really afford to spend or take time away from the family for selfish pursuits to alleviate depression. If they were not depressed, they could not justify what they consider selfishness.

Excuse to Quit

Yet another fringe benefit of depression is the rationale it affords for giving up. There are times when nearly everyone would like to quit trying; it would be so much easier to go away, relax, and let the world go by. One day I found myself in exactly this frame of mind.

I was involved in the development of a treatment program for seriously troubled youths. Early on, there was never enough money; trained staff were extremely difficult to find; the patients were rebellious and resistant to change. The cost in money, time, and energy seemed gigantic compared with the few good results I could identify. Surely I might as well find a place in the country and live off my garden. Had I allowed my thoughts to follow this line of reasoning, I know I would have become depressed with anger, helplessness, and futility that that involved.

Fortunately, I chose to recall the people we had helped. Youthful faces flashed into my mind. I knew from grateful letters and various sources that these young people and their entire families had benefited from our help. Before I knew it, my mood had been transformed from hopeless despair to gratitude for my opportunities to help and excitement over the dreams that were yet to be realized.

Attachment to a Therapist

Without doubt, the strongest person I have ever known was my father. I had no doubt that he could withstand any stress and cope with every problem that life was capable of dishing out. But even that invincible man once revealed a need when I was a little girl.

He had been telling me stories from his childhood on the plains of Kansas. In drinking from a pump in the bitterly cold winter, his tongue had once frozen to the icy metal of the pump spout. He had nearly lost his way in a blizzard but miraculously had seen the lights of the farm home and managed to return safely. His narrative stopped for a moment, and I quietly watched his brown eyes grow misty. Then, softly, he recited this verse,

> Turn backward, turn backward,
> Oh, Time in your flight!
> Make me a boy again
> Just for tonight.

He regained his composure, and I knew his strength was intact. But I also knew, through this rare moment of insight, that even the strongest people have secret inner pockets of vulnerability—times when they crave the protection of a strong, loving parent.

A therapist can assume this role in the heart of a depressed patient. Even though the patient becomes better and her depression recedes, this protective person can be so comforting that the patient prefers to keep coming for counseling, so she hangs on to her symptoms. A good, experienced counselor will be aware of the likelihood of dependency and will help the patient grow beyond it, meet some of her own needs, and look for a supportive network as well.

All of us need people for a variety of reasons. There are universal needs for acceptance, for laughter, for comfort and encouragement, and for advice and correction. To avoid future depression, I urge you to find a number of people who can offer you a resource for each of your needs. Call on them when you must and accept their help. Be certain, however, to return that favor with your assistance when they have needs.

Dependency on Medication

The ever-growing list of antidepressants offers great hope to depressed persons, but using them can be dangerous. In the complex biochemistry of our amazing bodies, drugs can create a physical dependency, and many people become psychologically dependent.

A patient once called me in panic from an airport. He had been detained through a flight change, but his bag was checked through to his destination. He was separated from those little pills. Physically, he could get along without them for long periods of time without difficulty—if they were in his medicine chest. But just knowing they were out of reach for a few hours threw him into terror. He was psychologically "hooked" on his pills.

Few, indeed, are persons who are *not* able to become either physically or psychologically dependent on prescription drugs. You may be one of those people who are staying depressed so you may enjoy the pleasurable feeling that chemical gives you. If that is true, please be honest about it. Ask your doctor to help you decrease it slowly until you are back under your own control again.

If, however, you are manic-depressive, schizophrenic, or one of those rare depressives who are truly chemically imbalanced, you may well need your prescription for life. Heart patients, diabetics, victims of high blood pressure, and others also need medication for life, much as they hate that fact. So be certain that you are under the care of a good physician and then trust his judgment.

The fringe benefits of depression are subtly tempting to pursue. Be very careful to avoid them. Keep searching for the real benefits of a truly healthy state of mind and emotion; you, too, can achieve that!

PREVENTION AND RECOVERY

The exciting news I have for you is this—you can overcome depression. You may need help from several sources, but the outcome is most likely to be positive!

There are several basic facts you need to understand. First is the importance of healthy self-esteem. You must believe that you are worthy of help and that you have the capability of finding and working with that help to overcome depression. If you lack self-esteem, begin to acquire it by listing all the good qualities you have. You need not become egotistical about yourself—in fact, facing your positive aspects can make you humble in a healthy sense. For each gift you have, there is someone to thank. As you discover, for example, a sense of humor, remember who taught that to you. Feel the gratitude such a memory will prompt and, if possible, let the person know your appreciation. Not only will this reinforce your self-esteem, but it also can reestablish bonds of friendship.

Do all you can do to reassess your personal worth, your achievements, and your goals by yourself. Seek affirmation from a relative or friend who will be honest with you. Read some helpful books and practice what you learn. Renew your faith and put it to work for you as well. Get proper exercise, a good diet, and adequate rest. Have a thorough physical examination.

If these tasks fail to bring you relief from your depression, by all means consult a good therapist. Even if you are single, I recommend that you find a counselor who understands family dynamics. You will benefit from seeing how you and your problems fit into your entire background. You are likely to need to forgive some of the people from your past, and recalling them will help you do so. If you are uncertain about the qualifications of a therapist, ask the therapist, a friend, your personal physician, or the professional organization to which he or she belongs. Once you settle on an individual, work cooperatively to establish confidence, gain insight, and follow through with recommendations. At any point that creates doubt, check out your questions and do not hesitate to seek a second opinion.

16

Self-Esteem

Confusion regarding values is rampant in our culture. When it became illegal to teach or practice religion in our public schools, most faculty members believed they were also forbidden to teach values. Parents were polarized by that law into those who supported it and those who made every effort to see its repeal. Many parents have lost faith in both their government, which was founded on religious freedom but now seems to be denying that, and their public schools. They see schools as an arm of the government they believe has betrayed them.

In my own metropolitan community, in the heart of the midwestern Bible Belt, the group of parents that is violently opposed to the teaching of values in schools fears any values taught would be those consistent with secular humanism and therefore totally erroneous. The other parent group adamantly stands by their belief that schools should stay away from any teaching that even touches on philosophy or religion. If there is a middle group, it is not vocal enough to be heard.

Because of this lengthy period in which the teaching of healthy values has been neglected, I fear we are seeing a severe loss of respect for life itself. And without that most basic respect, I seriously doubt that individuals can possess the vital quality of *self*-respect or self-esteem.

Within the last several months in my city, we have learned of three women who have given birth without the help of any other person, and in each case the mother killed her infant. In two cases the trials could result in prison sentences. One woman delivered her baby in an airline toilet; it drowned in the chemically treated toilet water, and the mother left it in a trash can at the next airport. She has been the object of the merciless glare of the media from coast to coast.

Because I was asked for an interview by a local television station, I thought very deeply about the possible reasons for such tragic wasting of life and for the lack of what I once believed to be the maternal instincts. A mother sheep or lion would carefully tend her new baby, nurse it, protect it, and raise it. Not so in the so-called higher animal—womankind.

I realized that our country has made it legal to destroy the life of a fetus up to twenty-four weeks of age. But we may send to prison the one who takes its life at forty weeks. This distinction was intended to make sense in terms of an infant's ability to live outside the womb, but the dividing line is very fuzzy.

The tragic truth is this—many signs in our society point to the broad-based devaluation of life itself. As people lose the essential values that give to life both direction and meaning, our entire culture suffers. Although the desperation of her plight may prompt a young woman to trash her own infant, it is not right!

I realize I am philosophizing a bit, because I am equally concerned about an extreme stand emerging in the religious world. More and more theologians in this school of thought are putting down the values of self-esteem and positive thinking. They relegate all psychotherapists to demonic dump heaps and say with incredible effrontery, "Just pray about your problems."

These men may not have encountered the countless people who say, "Pray? To whom? I can't even trust my dad. How can I pray to a god I've never seen? I *can't* believe in that stuff!" These are people I come to know as honestly groping ones who desperately want answers. They need intensive help to build relationships with a warm, loving, knowledgeable human, and then they will be ready to trust the God they *really* need. I believe it takes time to be ready for a spiritual birth just as it does for a human birth.

Perhaps the religionists who oppose the value of self-esteem are reacting to the egoists who pretend to need no resources beyond their own—either human or divine. Such people are not healthy, and no good psychotherapist would consider them to be. These people are likely to be narcissistic personalities, and we would try very hard to help them get better.

True enough, a positive mental attitude, alone or carried to an extreme, can deny the more negative truth and deprive persons of a realistic search for solutions to real problems. A positive mental attitude alone can become a rationalization that damages basic honesty.

But let's think through this dilemma of agnostic dehumanization and arrogant theology to that wonderful center of reality. If we are created in the very image of God (Genesis 1:27), as the Bible concisely asserts, we truly ought to enjoy self-esteem. It seems to me we negate His creatorship if we deny that. What we need to do is credit the Creator for the wonder of who He made us to be and not think we are great in and of ourselves.

In this context, self-esteem is the mirror of God's esteem of us. To humankind alone, of all God's creatures, were given the anatomy, the mental powers, and the spiritual bases for ruling the world. We've managed to mess things up rather badly, but that's because we've tried to go about it on our own, refusing the help we need—just as so many people do every day. We really dislike admitting weak spots and the need for help.

If a positive mental attitude is based on the certain knowledge of facts and is not a rationalization, it can be an asset par excellence! My positive thinking rests on the awareness that I have a powerful God who loves me and has promised the resources for living I need. I have, straight from Him, the amazing power of choice to use in deciding to understand and forgive myself and others so I needn't live in fear, pain, and guilt. In the very use of that power, I face the truth that I am *not* helpless. True enough, life has dealt me some fairly nasty blows over which I've had no control. But I've been able, through a positive attitude, to survive those blows with peace, courage, forgiveness, and love. I need never become depressed when I keep these facts clear.

Victor Frankl was right. His inspired insights taught that we have the ultimate power—to choose to make the best of the worst that life can dish out. And from our attitudes to our actions is but a tiny step of self-control.[1]

Self-esteem of a healthy sort, then, precludes most depression; conversely, the establishment of this self-esteem can help cure depression. Let me use a very personal example to tell you how you may set about remedying poor self-esteem.

When I reached the awesome age of forty, the time proverbially when life begins, I had to face some basic truths. I was working far too hard, I was enjoying life far too little, and I was becoming depressed. At the time I did not know what to do about these facts, but I was certain I would not spend the rest of my life being helpless in the vicious cycle of trying harder but failing more.

With the sort of help I so often prescribe, I gained the insights that were to change my life. Those changes have cured me of depression and connected me with the resources that have worked in the midst of immeasurable stress to hold me steady.

There were many delightful experiences in my childhood. There was time for games and laughter; I knew I was loved; I had great challenges to learn and explore; and I knew the incomparable value of hard work and achievement.

But I also experienced losses and grief. Early in life I learned to live with a type of criticism that would not allow me to feel really good about myself. Socially, I felt an outcast because of the strict religious rules by which my family lived.

Gradually and unconsciously I became critical of myself. No matter what I achieved, it was not enough. As I tried heroically to please people, I found that often those I served were complimen-

1. Victor Frankl, *Man's Search for Meaning* (New York: Simon and Schuster, 1984).

tary, so I tried even harder to acquire more appreciation. But no reward was enough. My inner feelings drove me to try harder to be even better and stronger. But by forty, I realized I could no longer keep up the pace. I became subclinically depressed. That means I knew despair, but I was able through monumental self-discipline to keep functioning. Few, if any, of those nearest me realized how I honestly felt.

When my very best efforts failed to make me feel better, I finally had to face the truth. I was depressed, and my depression was measured by the contrast between my inner world and my outer lifestyle. Outwardly I had achieved more success than almost any woman I knew. But inwardly I felt like the awkward, ugly, shy child I had once believed myself to be.

You see, my inner lack of self-esteem had driven me to try to prove to myself that I did have worth. But because of the degree of emptiness within me, all my efforts failed. Proving anything to the subconscious being is one of the most difficult, even futile, tasks in the world.

Painful as it was, I had to give up on my heroic efforts. I realized that I had to have help if I were to make the basic changes that would cure my depression. Against the advice of those who warned me that I would lose both my faith and my personal credibility, I carefully selected a therapist who was to help me achieve life-transforming inner health.

With a strange combination of trepidation and elation I traveled that two-year journey. I learned more than this book can hold, but acknowledging one fundamental fact became a turning point for me. My therapist said to me on my first visit, "You have more strength than you know!" Only because I knew him to be a man of impeccable integrity did I believe him. I certainly felt no strength— only helplessness. But I took hope from his perceptions of me, and that hope germinated in the healthier, more secure part of me that he had accurately discovered.

Each week I learned more about my inner being. I discovered a profound honesty about both my faults and my assets. I learned to correct some of my weaknesses and to accept some I couldn't change. I learned to respect and value the good things about myself, so my self-esteem began to solidify. I discovered that I didn't have to be perfect and that admitting my flaws enabled others to relate to me in a new and delightful camaraderie of sharing. I rediscovered a delightful sense of humor, and I value that ability to see lightness in even the most tense or painful situations. After years of practice at fitting the molds others modeled for me, I found a unique sense of individual creativity that is priceless. Even my spiritual life was revitalized as I began to understand that God had instilled all these qualities in me. I came to know that He saw I was imperfect and that He loved me—even more tenderly—because of (not in spite of) the flaws.

My relationship with others became more enjoyable than I had ever imagined. As I came to unconditional acceptance of myself, I was able to extend that to others. My children benefited from a mother who began to balance good training and discipline with a realistic appraisal of their possibilities and an unconditional acceptance of them.

Instead of relying on desperate attempts to *prove* my self-esteem and worth, I slowly became acquainted with the really beautiful *and* imperfect person I am. I'm still striving to grow and improve, but I really like this person (me) most of the time. When I receive criticism, I am no longer devastated by it (except rarely and momentarily). I would not knowingly hurt anyone in the world because I deeply respect life, yet I care very little if people disagree with me, nor do I worry about what they may think of me. My own self-respect and integrity have become my motivators and judge, as God enlightens them.

As I remind you of the component parts of depression, perhaps you can see how my journey led me out of this crippling state. First, knowing my core of strength, God-given, dispelled my old helplessness. Second, discovering my basic worth and realizing that was not neutralized by my flaws eliminated my guilt feelings. Third, recognizing the need for and learning how to accept myself and others unconditionally prevented most of the pain and fear of rejection. Fourth, realizing that I was not helpless and that I was safe from most pain released me from the anger that I had unconsciously carried. I do experience anger, but I know how to use it in a constructive manner instead of becoming enmeshed in its embittering old power.

How to Develop Self-Esteem

You may not need to go through months and years of psycho-analysis to develop healthy self-esteem. In fact, if you can follow these steps, I predict you can achieve it with only the help of your family and friends.

1. *Recognize your personal need* of reaching healthy self-esteem and come to the knowledge that it is permissible and possible. It is not egotism or "carnal" pride.

2. *Give up the fringe benefits of a negative self-image.* Little can be expected from a person who is not worth much, so you may slide through life more easily and with less risks if you continue to have a poor self-image. That is not a healthy way to live, however.

3. *Get rid of your guilt.* If you *are* guilty of wrongs you have not rectified, deal with that and make restitution. Ask forgiveness, accept it, and forgive yourself. If you *feel* guilty but you don't know of what you are guilty, or if the conduct of which you *feel* guilty is not actually wrong, seek clear information. Believe it, and let go of false guilt. Deal with guilt daily, and do not let it accumulate.

4. *Practice unconditional acceptance and love daily.* You can love others only as you love yourself, and you can hardly love at all unless you know God who is love. You must love yourself at your very worst if you are to acquire self-esteem. You will find it helpful to extend unconditional acceptance to those around you.

5. *Recognize and exercise your strength.* As you discover what you are good at (either at work or in leisure activities), practice

doing that as often as possible. Allow yourself to revel in your accomplishments while you work to improve them even more.

6. *Learn to separate who you are from what you do.* You may fail at a task, but that does not mean *you* are a failure. It may, instead, mean that you have courage enough to take a risk even if that may involve failure.

7. *Understand your anger.* It is my experience that anger is a defense against hurt feelings and it gives individuals a false sense of power. If you cling to your anger, it will cover your real pain and prevent your getting rid of it, and it will also hamper the development of genuine strength. To get rid of anger, name it, understand why you are angry, and decide what you will do about that.

8. *Deal with your pain.* You must face the hurts and resentments that have collected in your life. Take time to gather enough information to enable you to understand those who have hurt you, forgive them, and let go of your hurt feelings. Like anger, hurts can serve as a protection against further pain. But hanging on to hurt feelings can make you a martyr and prevent the development of self-esteem.

9. *Learn to live, forgiving.* This is not a showy, dramatic life-style, but a quiet, peaceful philosophy by which to live.

10. *Do something every day you can take pride in.* I don't mean that you must create a masterpiece or that you should brag to your family about your accomplishments. I mean that if you sweep the kitchen, you should do it in a fashion that brings satisfaction to you. The little things, done in your best style, will mirror to you the quality person you are.

11. In all these steps, *exercise your priceless power of choice.* You may decide a step is too difficult and eliminate it. That decision will delay your progress toward self-esteem. I urge you to

choose the self-discipline that will enable you to master the steps.

Build Self-Esteem in Children

I once read this statement, "It is in love, and through love, that one learns to accept himself—because another accepts him first." Once you have been loosed from the chains of depression, I hope you will know the profound truth of this quotation. As you learn the joy of self-esteem, I hope you will be moved to help others discover it as well.

It is especially important to practice self-esteem building with children. How many children would be tempted to use drugs or chemicals, to vandalize or steal, or to bully or abuse others if they felt really good about themselves? Almost all the serious conduct disorders of children and youths are their attempts to discover some sense of worth or to prove some level of power.

On airplanes flight attendants describe what to do in case there is a loss of air pressure. An oxygen mask, we are told, will drop down in front of us. We are told to attach the mask to our faces and strap its band about our heads. If we are traveling with a child, we are admonished to place our mask on first before attending to the child.

Being a parent, I feel that warning going against my protective instincts. I want to take care of the child first and then attend to myself. But my good reasoning tells me that I may pass out while attending my child and I would then be unable to function at all. So there are times to care for myself first. And building self-esteem is one of those times.

Once you have begun to establish your self-esteem, here are some rules to practice in extending that to your child.

1. *Develop an inner sense of unconditional acceptance of him.*
   Some aspect of his appearance or behavior may annoy you.
   Usually this feeling comes from your child's vague resemblance to some other person. Separate him from that person in
   your mind, and practice the unconditional acceptance you are
   learning for yourself.

2. *Practice communicating that acceptance* in the following ways: *(a)* give him direct eye contact in all interactions with him and make sure your eyes reveal your love; *(b)* give him the courtesy of listening to him and responding to what he says; *(c)* touch him in appropriate ways—gentle, playful, or protective—never mean or abusive; and *(d)* show him you crave time with him and use that time to share the activities, interests, and emotions of the day.

3. *Explore with her*. Help your child discover the talents and interests that are uniquely hers. Then help her develop those within the framework of her home and community. In such development, do not allow her to quit when the work becomes difficult. Help her achieve mastery.

4. *Assign responsibilities to her*. She will miss the thrill of achievement if you wait on her like a servant or complete her tasks for her when they seem tedious or difficult. Offer her help, encouragement, or firm insistence, but do not deprive her of learning her own competency.

5. *Accept his friends*. It may be difficult to share a cherished child with his peers. And it is frightening to see him entering a social world over which you have no control. It is healthy, however, for children to extend themselves to friendships that will balance and enrich their lives. Exercise caution and good judgment if you find your child's friends to be a really dangerous influence.

6. *Respect her ideas*. You will not always agree with her thinking, but you need not ridicule or harshly condemn her concepts. Discuss and debate with her, guide her to consider a range of possibilities, and quietly expect her to come to a place of clear thinking and sound values. This attitude will leave the door of communication open and will offer her the best opportunity to accept your positive-esteem building in due time.

7. *Respect and love her other parent* (as well as yourself!). This demands that you resolve disagreements, accept your spouse unconditionally, and avoid attempts to make him or her your rubber stamp. Even if you have suffered a divorce with its obvious disapproval and pain, find a way to understand and forgive. Then reestablish a friendship with that person so your child will not have to choose between you or believe that he is bad in the ways that resemble the other parent.

8. *Practice positive training and discipline.* All youngsters will test the limits of authority; they will assert their wills; and they will be accidentally or deliberately destructive at times. Children must learn to adapt to the needs and respond respectfully to the feelings of others.

   You can teach these qualities through shame and guilt, destroying your child's self-esteem and implanting the seeds of depression or rebellion. Or you can teach her with a meaningful example, clearly defined rules, and loving but firm consequences. You need never label your child, place guilt on her, or abuse her to train and discipline her effectively.

9. *Consistently express your approval and pleasure.* How easy it is to save energy for the necessary discipline about misbehaviors and overlook all the really commendable things a child does. The positive behaviors cause no pain, and because of that fact, parents so easily take them for granted. Develop an affirming attitude. Express appreciation simply, genuinely, and frequently. Tell your spouse something good about your child, and compliment him whenever he deserves it.

10. *Teach and demonstrate forgiveness.* There is a powerful paradox in asking your child, "Please forgive me! I was too hasty in my judgment. I was wrong!" It may sound weak, and you may fear your child will lose respect. But the exact opposite is true. Your child knows when you are in the wrong, and she will respect you infinitely more when you demonstrate the wis-

dom and courage to admit it. It will become routine, then, for her to admit wrongs and seek forgiveness.

11. *Practice beauty.* Teach your child to revel in the beauty of nature. Make your home, no matter how modest it may be, as lovely as you can. A green plant or wild flower can make any table beautiful.

Keep yourself clean, well-groomed, and as tastefully dressed as you can. Doing this requires careful choices more than lots of money. Help your child to look his best. He does *not* need designer-labeled clothes, but colors and fabrics that go with his complexion and suit his personality can make a positive difference in how he feels about himself. And he needs to hear from you that he has chosen wisely as he learns to express his inner beauty in his outward appearance.

12. *Realize that your child has a mission in life.* One of the best legacies you can leave your child is the sure knowledge that she is alive for a purpose. She can do something in this world that no one else will do. Discuss this philosophy at times, keep her awareness focused on discovering her goals, and assist her in reaching them. Perhaps nothing else can weave such deep meaning into a child's life.

If you will follow these rules with reasonable consistency, I can guarantee you will raise a child with healthy self-esteem. The results are so rewarding you will be glad of every bit of energy you have expended.

Build Self-Esteem in Other Adults

You have just read the guidelines for strengthening your own self-esteem and how to build self-esteem in your child. Most of us live or work with adults daily who also need assistance in this important compartment of their lives.

You certainly are not responsible for convincing them they

need to change—valid as that need is. However, you *are* responsible for avoiding any damage to such people. A much-loved professor of mine as I studied pediatrics made frequent wise statements. One of these was, "We may at first not know why a child is sick or how to treat him. In the process of finding out, our foremost goal must be that we will at least not hurt him!" That is true in all life's relationships. Once you have learned the joy of personal self-worth, you will want to share that with others. Here are some guidelines for doing so:

- *Carefully develop a loving, honest attitude.* You will thus be able to avoid criticisms and put-downs that can further destroy self-esteem. If your honesty demands some critical comment, you can do that in such a loving way that it helps the other person. Instead of "What a sloppy job!" try, "I know you can do better. Let me help."

- *Find something good in all situations—even the worst.* Perhaps the only good in someone's mistake may be a lesson learned. That is enough to restore hope and prevent further erosion of that essential self-esteem.

- *Cultivate the quality of sincerity.* If you compliment a friend when that is not valid, the friend will be unable to trust you. Do give compliments when you sincerely mean them. Instead of "That outfit looks great on you!" when, in fact, it doesn't, say "That color really accents your deep-blue eyes!"

- *Let the person know you value her.* It takes time for a phone call, a note, or a luncheon date. But that's what it takes to let anyone know you like her—that she is *worth* liking.

- *Ask for a favor you need.* Giving is truly easier than needing. But when you ask another to help you, you are really saying, "You are a loving and caring person and I can trust you to meet my need." What an ego boost that may be.

- *Tell another person something good about your friend.* All too often, people reverse this principle and repeat negative things. By telling a mutual acquaintance a positive event, you are likely to raise the respect of that individual for your friend, and this increases his self-respect.

- *Respond to the likes and dislikes of your friend.* I felt extremely important recently when my daughter unexpectedly stopped in with my favorite flavor of frozen yogurt. Thoughtful remembrances say, "You are important!"

- *Offer resources for help.* At some point, your friend may discover he needs help to build self-esteem. Be prepared for that time with a few well-chosen names of professionals who can provide that service.

- *Share your own weaknesses.* Perhaps nothing is as comforting, or offers as much hope to someone who is down, as revealing some experience of your own. By discussing how you have grown in self-esteem, you may offer just the hope a friend needs.

In a world that seems to be heartless and mechanistic, I hope you will develop the habit of caring about others—how they feel and what they need. In reaching out to them in a loving, constructive manner, I can assure you that you and they will be better people.

17

Self-Help

Susan, the single mother who shared her experiences in the chapter on loneliness, was an example of someone who conquered grief and depression by herself. She not only found her way out of the black pit of despair but also managed to stay out. When she was once again threatened by depression, she discovered how to keep it from becoming incapacitating.

Let's review the steps she took so that you, too, may prevent depression from overwhelming you.

1. *Recognize depression.* If you have ever experienced depression or even grief, you are more likely to recognize its reappearance at its first sign. If not, review the signs and symptoms of depression at the end of chapter five. If you suspect you are becoming depressed, do not ignore the fact. Go on to step two.

2. *Explore the reasons for it.* Susan knew promptly that the reason for her depression lay in the loss of a love relationship for the second time. Many people are unable to pinpoint the reasons for

their problems so quickly, and some find it almost impossible. I have discovered, however, that only a little help can uncover the onset as well as the factors that precipitated it *if* they have not allowed it to go on too long.

Many times a fairly minor event in the present resembles a major tragedy from the past and hurls people into the helplessness of a bout of depression. Sometimes if you will focus on the emotion you are experiencing, you will identify its precursor, realize that you survived that event, and find the solution to your present problem.

Talking with a friend will often enable you to clarify your thoughts and feelings and help you find the answers you need. Be certain to choose a person you can trust.

3. *Make decisions.* Once you understand the reasons for your depression, you will be ready to do something about it. You may need to unload some of your responsibilities or seek advice in smoothing trouble spots in your life. Deciding what to do will begin to lift you out of the sense of helplessness and futility that is a large part of depression.

4. *Take action.* Decisions are important and become the turning points in life. But decisions alone are not enough. You must take action and follow through with the course your decisions map out.

5. *Seek encouragement.* All of us need help at times, and frankly, people who are secure enough to admit it get along best. You will certainly be able to give help to others when you know how beneficial it has been to you.

6. *Accomplish something daily.* When you can retire at night with even one job well done, you will know your life is not in vain. Even small achievements will reflect the worth you cannot feel while you are down.

7. *Think positively.* Focus on decisions, activities, and accomplishments. You can multiply bad feelings and create a state of despair

simply by concentrating on negative feelings and fearful, suspicious ideas. Keep your energy for thinking of whatever is just, lovely, and of good report.

Primary Prevention

If you are fortunate enough to be the parent of a young child, you are in a prized position. You can raise your child to be so emotionally healthy that depression will be less likely to occur. Here are some additional guidelines. We have discussed them earlier, but they are worth repeating.

1. *Accept your child unconditionally.* It does not matter that you wanted a boy and had a girl, nor does it matter that she inherited Aunt Mathilda's big nose or Uncle Harry's grouchy disposition (which is probably not true!). Open your eyes to her unique beauty, and love her as much as you can. Give your child wholesome parental affection; protect her from harm but let her grow and learn to explore; teach her to respect herself and others through loving correction. Give her your undivided attention, and show that by stopping your activities to look at her, listen to her, and respond.

2. *Be proud of your child.* I'm not thinking of the egotistical pride that tries to *make* your child superior to all others. But each child needs the quiet confidence that, to you at least, he *is* the dearest of people. When he does anything worthy of praise, compliment him calmly and simply—and really mean it. If he is stubborn and difficult, be firm and set limits in a kind but unyielding manner. When he gives in as he must at times or regains control, let him know you are proud of his efforts.

3. *Spend time with your child.* Yes, it's true, quality counts more than quantity. But there must be enough time to communicate the best quality, or your child will not benefit from it. Find some activities, both work and play, that you can enjoyably share with your child and do those regularly.

4. *Avoid anger, shame, or abuse*. You need not use these extremes to train or discipline your child. Practice self-control before you try to teach your child to control herself. Show her how by your actions, and then she will understand your words.

5. *Laugh with your child*. Avoid laughing *at* your child. But look for funny jokes to share, or plan some play activities that provide fun together.

6. *Be predictable and consistent*. In a given type of situation, try to react in the same way each time it occurs. You will react differently to various events and behaviors, but be as consistent as possible within the framework of any single happening.

7. *Share your values and beliefs*. One of the main strengths of healthy families is that of practicing religious beliefs as a family. Find and clarify your set of values, discuss them, try to live by them, and make them so appealing that your child will adopt them, too.

8. *Relinquish your hold on your child*. Developing into a strong, independent adult takes a long time. Allow your child to learn to walk alone when you are still nearby to protect him and help him get going again if he falls. Determine the child's capability and readiness for new independence. Then invite and encourage him to assume this responsibility with your blessing.

9. *Be there for your child*. No matter how old we get, it's natural to yearn at times for a parent's love, comfort, and wisdom. If you can find a way to offer these without controlling or interfering, you will provide a priceless defense against depression. Life is never utterly hopeless as long as someone honestly cares and can communicate that caring in practical ways. Budget your time and energy wisely, and keep your priorities in order so you can be available when your child needs you.

10. *Communicate*. When people can talk about their problems and feelings, they are much more likely to work them out and avoid depression. Yet for many people this is difficult, and they somehow do not get around to dealing with stresses. To prevent depression, talk about whatever bothers you and encourage your child to follow suit. (This works for adults as well as children.)

If your child is older and you did not know some of the steps to take early on to prevent depression, begin now. You can make amends for past mistakes and strengthen your child from this point. Let her know how much you love her and how sorry you are for your mistakes. And then move on. You and your child can prevent depression.

18

Professional Treatment

As you can readily see from what I've discussed throughout this book, depression is quite complex. Some forms of treatment are more effective than others in certain cases. To guide you in making well-informed decisions about what kind of treatment to seek, I'll explain something about the various forms available. I'll also caution you about some risks of poor psychotherapy. But perhaps the most important thing for you to remember is that there is help (and hope) for you if you are depressed.

Medication

Exciting new information has been acquired by the technology and knowledge explosion of modern medical science. Many brilliant researchers have become convinced that undertaking intricate diagnostic procedures is the first step toward treatment. The second (and all too often last) step is pinpointing a precise medication that will reestablish perfect hormonal and biochemical balance.

They carefully determine dosages and observe interactions of the chemicals. Voilà! The person is cured!

But is he, in fact, cured so easily? My experience reveals that in many cases, he is not. Over time, his body seems to build up a tolerance for the medicine, and he needs larger doses. Sooner or later, he will probably demand a different medicine. Over the years, even with the steady stream of new and better chemicals, some people no longer feel as good as they would like. Their depression grows despite the medicine.

If depression occurs as a reaction to temporary stress, it may improve by itself. Depression may occur, for example, over a poor job evaluation. With some extra training or supervision, that person improves. She knows she is doing better, her fellow workers recognize her improvement, and her next evaluation verifies that her supervisor is pleased. She is no longer depressed. I fear that medical science alone may get the credit for such improvement in depression. It would have improved anyway because it occurred as a response by a somewhat insecure person to a naturally time-limited stress factor.

Actually that situation may not need any outside intervention. If the victim of *reactive depression* thinks carefully about her life and discovers the problems that are creating stress, she can formulate a plan to solve the problems. Putting that plan into effect, then, can indeed work, giving her the thrill of achieving success and confidence in being even more capable of solving the next issue.

Reactive depression is a psychiatric diagnosis describing a state of more or less temporary depression that occurs in response to some stress factor. This sort of depression, in my experience, is more likely to be grief or closely akin to it. The symptoms of depression, however, are present, and many people who suffer in this way require professional help.

You may consider me a traitor to my profession as you read my concerns about the purely medical treatment of depression. Please understand that I am immensely excited about the research and the production of medicines that save lives and increase well-being for countless people. I am troubled, however, about a growing number of physicians who seem to believe that pills alone are enough to cure depression.

In my opinion three situations in depressive illness really demand medication.

1. *The person is suicidal.* Extremely severe depression is a vicious cycle. The individual's helplessness makes her give up. Her lack of functioning convinces her that she is truly helpless. Frustration over the helplessness traps her, and she expects someone else to take care of her. When that does not happen, she spirals downward to total despair. She finally believes there is no hope. Rather than continue to live in pain, she may become convinced that suicide is the only way out. Medication can save the life of such a person. It is a sign that, at last, someone is *trying* to help, and the proper medicine also relieves emotional distress and restores hope.

   It is, however, extemely important to set up a team of people to protect a seriously depressed person. If a family member is suicidal, I suggest that you offer to keep the medication to avoid the likelihood of an overdose. Be observant in a lovingly protective manner to be sure that the medicine is taken properly and that other facets of the person's life are as positive as possible. And keep in touch with both your loved one and her physician (of course, with her knowledge and consent) to be sure the medicine is working as it should. It is my opinion that any truly suicidal person needs the protection of being in a hospital until the risk of self-damage is past.

2. *The person cannot function normally.* Even though reactive depression is time limited, that time may be too long to endure. A graduate student studying for comprehensive exams knows they will be over in six weeks, for example. But his confidence level is low and anxiety runs high. He learns of a friend who didn't pass and vaguely recalls a year in high school when he experienced some failures. He can't sleep well and finds he is gaining weight because he snacks too much. He cannot concentrate and forgets information he knew well.

This person deserves help, and proper medication can see him through that difficult time without so much anxiety and its accompanying depression. He needs to be aware, however, that the medication can make him feel so good that it will be tempting to keep on taking it even when the exams are over. Or he may find it tempting to get a refill when the next stress hits, even if he knows he could handle it on his own.

Since physicians are convinced about the acceptability of medication, many find it easier to administer medicine than to guide their patients to seek good psychotherapy. When patients demand it, they often prescribe pills too easily. I know a number of people who get prescriptions from several doctors. They self-medicate, they take too much, and before they know it, they are addicted. Please take this warning seriously. You are as much to blame as your physician if you become drug-dependent—and more so if you fail to be honest about getting medication from more than one physician.

3. *Other help is in the process of taking effect.* I have worked with a number of patients over the years who refused medication because they were afraid of becoming drug-dependent. They were quite willing to work regularly in psychotherapy, but they suffered needless weeks of distress that could have been alleviated by proper amounts of the right medication. Taking properly prescribed pills can make therapy more effective and save unnecessary pain.

Electroshock Therapy

Long before medical science discovered the earliest chemicals to use for depression, psychiatrists found that passing a mild electric current through the brain almost miraculously brought about dramatic improvement. The patient experienced some loss of memory for a time but had very few other bad effects. Unfortunately, the improvement did not last indefinitely, and in some weeks or months the patient would require another treatment.

As medicines and psychotherapy were discovered and refined,

shock therapy fell into disuse, and its use has been greatly decreased. However, it is a technique you need to know about, because it may be remarkably helpful in a few cases.

If you have tried everything else without improvement, consider this treatment. Some people, usually older but not always, experience no relief from even the best medicine. They are unable to change their beliefs, let alone control their feelings or grasp the opportunity to improve their self-concept. They can accept no encouragement or reassurance from anyone. Not only are these rare individuals miserable, but they can make life for those around them unbearable.

For these unfortunate persons, electroshock therapy offers genuine hope. The treatments once were somewhat unpleasant. I assisted with many of them when I was serving my medical internship some thirty years ago. Now, however, the technique is very different. A mild sedative or anesthetic is administered, the current is applied extremely briefly and carefully, and the patient sleeps for a few hours. Very few now seem to have memory lapses, and those are quite temporary. The relief from the anguishing depression is dramatic.

Of those who have such treatment, many can be further relieved by proper medication and psychotherapy. For some reason these remedies become more effective than they were before the treatment.

Psychotherapy

Many forms of psychotherapy are available to those who suffer from depression. These have in common the awareness of stress and its impact on feelings, actions, and thought processes. But each form approaches these dynamics from different angles. Let me explain briefly what these schools of thought are about.

Cognitive Therapy

This form of counseling attempts to teach depressed people new methods of thinking and coping with life. It does not work on feelings as much as it does on choosing, disciplining the self, collecting accurate information, and finding out how to take control of life.

To be successful, this therapy demands a trusting relationship between therapist and patient. Otherwise he would discount the therapist when they disagreed and would be afraid to explore new ideas or try different methods. The therapist must know information accurately, must be profoundly honest with the patient, and must be able to think with the patient. He must be able to approach problems from the patient's perspective, yet incorporate the new ideas and objectivity that the patient needs.

A friend of mine who has known severe depression says that depressed people have "crooked thinking." That is an excellent description. The way problems and the world itself seem when people are down is not, in fact, the way they are. Cognitive therapy sets disturbed perceptions straight.

Furthermore, it demands that the patient be able to find some energy with which to collaborate with the counseling. It is rare, but I have seen a few depressed people who were so "down" they truly could not think well and could not benefit from cognitive therapy.

For milder cases, however, and for the person who can trust both herself and her counselor, this can be wonderfully effective. Seeing a person, who has believed she is totally powerless, discover amazing strength in herself is pure joy to a therapist. And watching her use those discoveries to stop being depressed and learn to enjoy life makes my profession most rewarding.

Analytic Therapy

Many years ago Sigmund Freud discovered a remarkable connection between present problems and past experiences. The events of early childhood, he believed, left their imprint on adult perceptions and feelings but were often repressed into the unconscious self. He believed that sexual feelings and experiences, struggling through that unconscious state, were especially powerful in their impact on adult functioning. In order, therefore, to free patients from their neuroses, he believed they must recall memories of at least the most significant of such events. He found that by recapturing these elusive memories, patients could understand their present feelings, could become free from anxieties, and were able to function in a far healthier manner.

For many decades a great many psychiatrists closely followed Freud's principles. His techniques were tedious and extremely costly in time and money. But until more was learned about the physical and biochemical aspects of depression, his principles were, some people believe, the best guidelines therapists had.

Two well-known students of Freud who promoted variations of his principles were Alfred Adler and Carl Jung. Jung has been especially valued because of his emphasis on the spiritual aspects of life.

Freud's ideas provide great insight and are helpful in today's complex society in understanding mental and emotional illnesses. But many excellent psychotherapists have come to disagree with psychoanalysis as a primary mode of treatment, and many no longer use it at all.

Reality Therapy/Control Theory

A favorite of mine among present-day psychiatrists is Dr. William Glasser. He is perhaps best known for his book, *Reality Therapy,* in which he proposes that natural consequences are the best therapy of all. When anyone makes a poor decision or acts in an irresponsible or foolish manner, certain results are bound to reveal the mistakes that were made.

Often, well-meaning adults rescue children or each other from bad results. Some parents, for example, allow their children to watch TV or play rather than study in the evenings. Due to poor study habits, the youngsters make low grades on examinations at school. Rather than allow the bad grades to motivate the children to remedy their time management and self-discipline, the parents may attempt to get the teacher to raise the grade, give an easier test, or at least allow some extra work to improve the children's academic standing. I have even known irate parents to threaten to have a teacher fired if he did not raise a child's marks.

On the other hand, parents may become extremely rigid and demanding of their children. They remind them constantly that it is time to feed the pets, mow the grass, or clean their rooms. Children naturally are a bit lazy, but with constant nagging they also become angry. They come to have intensely mixed feelings of love and resentment toward their parents. This dilemma, with its inner conflict, creates great depression in children who feel guilty, sad, helpless, and angry. They become afraid and worried about themselves and their parents.

Dr. Glasser guides parents and teachers in helping children by establishing a plan of action. They work together to decide what is a reasonable level of responsibility, and then the children choose a consequence that is most likely to help them remember the task the next time and follow through with it.

For many decades, Dr. Glasser teaches, psychotherapists have tried to help people identify their hidden feelings and attitudes. The idea behind this is that once people understand their feelings, they can then recognize their needs and make the decisions that will relieve those bad feelings. Instead, says Dr. Glasser, people need to collect accurate information and make good decisions. They must discipline or control their behavior, then their feelings will become more positive and their outlook on the world will almost certainly improve.

I have heard that people who are depressed will feel better if they accomplish just one task each day. That job may be as simple as making the bed or seeing to it that all the dirty dishes are cleaned up and put away. I have tried this, even though I am not depressed, and agree that it is a great feeling to leave my bedroom and kitchen neat when I go to work in the morning. It is especially comforting to return to an uncluttered home after a long, hard day!

When you learn from your mistakes (reality therapy) and assume the responsibility of making wise decisions for yourself (taking control), you simply cannot feel helpless. It is less likely that you will feel sad or angry, and your guilt feelings are almost certain to decrease. Thus, nearly every feeling that comprises depression will improve through living this way.

Family Systems Theory

For many years a number of mental health specialists have realized the impact of the entire family on a single person who suffers from depression or other emotional problems. They call the person who is suffering an illness the *identified patient*. This implies that others within the family are equally troubled but are able to cover their symptoms and to function reasonably successfully.

Some researchers believe the identified patient serves the role of scapegoat. He takes on the problems of the family and often is the one who first is responsible for getting help. An example of this is a young adult single mother I worked with many years ago. She had discovered that her bickering parents fought much less when she got into trouble. They would rally their energy and focus on helping their "struggling" child. At the point of their serious threatening of a divorce, this *almost*-heroic teenager became pregnant. She believed her worst of all possible situations might save their marriage and preserve the family. And so it did—for a time.

Family systems therapists wisely work at correcting the mis-communications and imbalances in the entire family's functioning that contribute to the person's problems. At the same time they help the identified patient work through the situation.

Behavior Modification

This concept is based on the theory that behavior is what counts in life and that behaviors are learned and become habits. This theory, then, teaches that depression is simply a learned habit or the result of such habits. Therefore, changing the habits of acting and reacting will free the victim from his depression.

If a person is trained to behave respectfully, she will, in time, come to feel respectful. Then her actions and feelings will correlate, and she will be a better person.

There is some truth in this theory, and all of us are likely to feel better if we smile at people and they smile back. For truly depressed persons, however, this is not the total answer. I have seen persons who were treated by well-trained experts in behavior modification act out the anger of their depression in violent ways. This concept, in my opinion, is a wonderful skill to develop and use in conjunction with another mode of treatment that enhances total insight.

Transactional Analysis

In the very early 1960s Dr. Eric Berne, a practicing psychoanalyst, revised the vocabulary and many of the concepts of Freud's psychoanalytic theory. In working with patients he discovered that they would talk and act like children at times, but at other times, they sounded like angry parents. At still other periods, they could be logical and unemotional.

Dr. Berne changed the old terminology for the personality from Freud's well-known ego, superego, and id to simple, meaningful words. The ego became *the Adult* because it can think logically, decide wisely, and function effectively.

The superego became *the Parent* because while it served as the conscience, it was trained by the individual's parents. It could be critical or nurturing; these roles could be healthy, or if they got out of balance, they could emotionally damage the individual or others.

To Dr. Freud, the unconscious part of the personality was the id. Dr. Berne redefined it as *the Child* and further subdivided it into the free or natural child and the adaptive child. This part of the personality expresses feelings and needs either freely or with restraint, depending upon early training.

How the individual transacts within the self, Dr. Berne taught, enables him to function more or less successfully. If the Parent (conscience) is too rigid or harsh, he is likely to feel too restricted and may become very depressed. If the Parent is too lenient, he may do all sorts of wrongs and never feel a twinge of healthy guilt that could set him right.

Furthermore, how he communicates or transacts with others is determined by his ego state and that of others. If he habitually communicates as a critical, harsh Parent, those around him are likely to act like frightened children—they will either comply or rebel!

In this mode of treatment, therefore, the therapist teaches a patient to analyze himself first and then others. He learns to choose which ego state to use as he recognizes the ego state of another person. The therapy also helps the patient learn to resolve inner conflicts between the Child wishes and feelings and the Parent demands and restrictions.

As the individual learns this logic with its inherent strength, the helplessness, guilt, and anger of depression can be improved fairly readily. As in all psychotherapy, it is extremely important for him to be honest with himself, to avoid blaming the parents who formed those early habits, and to assume responsibility in establishing new and healthy balances in ego-state functioning.

Gestalt Therapy

In contrast to the more analytical approach of many schools of psychology, Gestalt theory proposes that all experience consists of a whole response by a person to a situation. This response is a complete entity rather than the sum of reactions to specific elements in a situation. Many people react to life in a divided or ambivalent fashion. Gestalt therapy attempts to reunify or integrate the feelings and thinking of patients and create, or restore, that wholeness—the *Gestalt*.

The proponents of this therapy will often use physical symptoms in their treatment. For example, if someone has a stiff neck, she is asked to deliberately tighten all the muscles in her neck as much as she can. After holding the entire neck rigidly, she is instructed to relax until the stiffness is gone. I have seen these techniques actually relieve neck pain, and then the sufferer can define the stress that may have precipitated the pain. Just as she learned to control the pain of the stiff neck, she can discover how to control the stress behind it.

Again, I hope you can see that in skillful hands a cooperative patient can discover her strength (eliminating helplessness), use this to resolve pain (relieving anger and sadness), and learn to take healthy charge of her life and relationships.

Biofeedback

In recent years, researchers in human sciences have discovered that people have more control over their bodies than they once believed. By concentration, they can dilute blood capillaries, lower blood pressure, and slow the heart rate, for example. With training, they can also control the body's reaction to stress so that anxiety decreases and depression is less likely to develop.

Within recent months, I have read books by devoted religious authors who believe this is evil, but I can find no reason for that idea. It is simply learning to control that part of the nervous system (called the involuntary or sympathetic system) which was once believed to be beyond control. And by that control, a person's entire well-being can be improved.

Other Forms of Therapy

Other forms of therapy are too numerous to elaborate upon in detail. The concepts of Carl Rogers are embodied in his well-defined client-centered therapy; the therapist mainly reflects to the patient his own feelings or statements so as to help him understand himself better.

Logo therapy is a concept developed by Victor Frankl. Out of his suffering and that of millions of other prisoners at Auschwitz, he discovered that one power within us can never be taken away. That power is the capacity to choose how we will feel and react to the vicissitudes of life. As I mentioned earlier, this, too, is a powerful weapon to use against the helpless anger and sadness of depression.

A friend of mine who lives with immense stress has undergone extensive psychotherapy. He told me that he learned a great deal from this process, but the most significant fact of all was this—*he had the power to choose.* He could decide how to handle what life threw at him. He could give in to anger or helplessness, or he could choose to work out the problems, regain inner peace, and react in a loving, constructive manner. I suspect the very fact he is alive today rests on this truth.

Where to Turn for Help

If you are seriously depressed by your own definition or according to the symptoms given in this book, you may well need some professional help. Here are some guidelines to enable you to choose the sort of therapy that will most quickly and effectively promote your recovery.

1. *When to choose a psychiatrist.* I recommend a psychiatrist (a medical doctor who specializes in psychotherapy) if you have the following elements in your condition: *(a)* you are unable to sleep well and are becoming exhausted; *(b)* your appetite is excessive, or you have lost all interest in food; *(c)* you are having serious difficulty with your memory and/or your ability to think clearly and make decisions wisely; *(d)* you are experiencing great difficulty in carrying on a conversation with your family and friends, and you can hardly recall when you last had a good laugh; *(e)* you feel your job may be in jeopardy; and *(f)* if you are seriously thinking of suicide or have ever tried to hurt yourself or take your life.

   A psychiatrist can offer carefully selected and supervised medications. This will soon restore you to fairly healthy functioning. If you are truly suicidal or so depressed you can't function normally at all, a psychiatrist can admit you to a hospital. You may receive expert care there until you are capable of making it on your own. Please do *not* hesitate to cooperate with this recommendation. It could save your life!

   A caution, however, is vitally important. Do not settle for simply feeling better. As you improve, you will find the energy to dig into your habit patterns and the early events that formed them. You can then discover what made you so depressed, what caused the hurts that you learned to cover up with anger, and what convinced you that you are so helpless.

   Once you have the answers to those questions, you are much less likely to become depressed again. You will be prepared to understand and overcome the stress and hurts that so quickly turn to anger, making you feel guilty, helpless, and hopeless.

2. *When to choose a counselor.* You will find a therapist from any of the philosophies discussed above to be helpful under the following circumstances: *(a)* if you are not suicidal, can think clearly enough to work with a psychotherapist, and are sleeping well; *(b)* if you have a physician who can prescribe and monitor any needed medications while you are working through the

counseling process; and *(c)* if you can find a therapist who understands the physical components of depression and is willing to work with a medical doctor when this input is needed.

It is not necessary to agree with your therapist in every detail, whatever her background may be, to receive help. It is essential, however, that you both maintain open minds, mutual respect, and a willingness to work together in areas that do seem logical and feel like they fit you and your situation.

What Credentials Are Important

To be certain that you find the best counselor for you, here are some explanations of the various disciplines.

Social workers. Social work counselors must have at least an M.S.W. degree. In other words they have completed college and two years beyond that and have a master of social work degree. This means they have spent about one year in counseling people under the supervision of an experienced, well-qualified person.

People who have received additional training and are qualified to supervise others have the letters A.C.S.W. after their names as well as, or instead of, M.S.W. The A.C.S.W. means they are members of the national Academy of Certified Social Workers. They may be no better counselors but they have more training and experience.

It is rare to find people with a doctorate in social work unless they are professors or research workers in a university.

Social workers are especially skilled through training to understand the impact of families and society in general on the problems of their clients. They are helpful in bringing into focus the events that have influenced self-image and perceptions of life.

Psychologists. The minimal training that qualifies psychologists to work as counselors is that of a master's degree. This degree is conferred on people who have completed college and an additional year or two of study and supervised counseling. Many people with such training are excellent therapists.

A great many psychologists go beyond the master's degree for a Ph.D., which requires at least three additional years of study. The training includes concepts regarding research and the acquisition of new and better modes of understanding and treating mental illnesses. It includes more supervised counseling and the training to become a supervisor. It demands an extensive study and research project (more complex than the thesis demanded of master's level students), so you can see these persons are well qualified to treat depression.

The confusion in the broad spectrum of psychology lies in the varied philosophies it includes. Psychologists may be skilled in one or more of these fields: behavioral psychology; educational psychology; cognitive therapy; Jungian therapy; Adlerian therapy; psychoanalysis (Freudian); reality therapy; family systems therapy (Bowen, Menuchin, and others); Rogerian psychology; transactional analysis; Gestalt therapy; developmental psychology; logo therapy; and biofeedback. Others are not as commonly used and are too numerous to mention.

Most psychologists understand nearly all these specialties and can usually work well with several. The philosophy to choose will depend on you and your specific symptoms and ways of looking at life. It also depends on the experience of the therapist and the concepts he has used most successfully. Frankly, I know of no good guidelines by which you can select from this catalog. I truly believe your relationship with and trust in your therapist are most important of all.

Psychiatrists. These medical or osteopathic doctors have usually completed four years of college, four years of medical school, and three to four years of additional training (a residency) in the specific study of neurology and psychiatry. They must have passed several sets of rigorous examinations and have worked under close supervision during most or all of their training.

At one time most psychiatric training was based upon Freud's analytic concept, but this has changed greatly. The developments and discoveries of biochemical research have made most physicians aware of the impact of stress on the body's endocrine system and the influence of these chemicals on the functioning of the brain and the nervous system.

The field of psychiatry now is divided into the organically oriented physicians and those who were recently derided by one psychiatrist as "talking doctors." The "talking doctors," like psychologists, are further subdivided into a variety of philosophies that are similar to those listed above. Most doctors use a combination of medication and psychotherapy and usually will work, in part, with a team composed of a social worker, a psychologist, and sometimes a nutritionist, a neurologist, or an occupational therapist or music therapist.

As I explained earlier, a few patients will benefit from electroshock therapy. It will certainly require a highly trained specialist to perform this sort of treatment, and only a few psychiatrists maintain the skills through experience.

What Are the Dangers?

Good psychotherapy has so many benefits that I hate to even mention the risks. But in all fairness and honesty, I must. The risks can be easily cataloged into three groups: (1) physical, (2) mental, and (3) moral or spiritual.

Physical Risks

These risks are present with *any* therapist when a person has a primarily mental or emotional problem as in depression. The risks are magnified when a person does not maintain good medical care and when he chooses a therapist who is not medically trained.

If you consult with a social worker or psychologist, have a thorough physical examination. Be certain your nutritional state is good, your thyroid functions well, and you are not anemic. Have your doctor check you for any mild chronic illness that could make you *feel* depressed but actually stems from a physical cause. Be certain you have nothing wrong with your neurological system.

When you are given any medication, ask your doctor if you should expect any reactions. Many medicines that relieve depression may make you drowsy or even tense and excited. These reactions are usually transient, but you must avoid driving or doing potentially hazardous work during this time.

Avoid becoming dependent on your medication. Your doctor

should explain how long you may need the pills. It may vary from a few weeks to a lifetime. When your stress becomes less, see if your doctor will agree to your going off or decreasing the medicine for a time. A few friends have surprised me. They have become able to handle stress in their lives without medicine when, by all expert opinions, they should not have been able to do so.

If you are a depressed person who prefers to find and pursue the easiest course in life, you may discover you like medication and its effect. You swallow a pill and are relieved of most pain and sadness for several hours. You may look for excuses to stay on these magical pills.

Let me urge you to resist this impulse. I have seen patients who had been on medication they no longer needed but learned to lean upon. When they finally decided to stop the useless dependency, they endured true anguish for some time—both physical and mental. Tempting as it is, don't set yourself up for such distress. When you and your physician feel you can stop the medicine, do so at once!

Mental Risks

For years, I have studied and basically believed in good psychotherapy. And I still do. But I have heard from several patients in recent months who have raised the red flag of "danger" in my awareness.

One patient was influenced by a therapist who actually had many unresolved conflicts of her own. She made unfounded and untrue comments about this patient's spouse. The doubts and suspicions she created in a few brief sessions have taken years to overcome. Obviously, she was trying to make herself appear better than the patient's spouse, but instead she damaged the trust and intimacy of a strong marriage.

Several other patients of mine have been negatively influenced by group therapy. Basically healthy ideas and thinking were challenged so strongly by these groups that the individual decided *they* must be wrong and changed their very accurate personal perceptions.

Group therapy has great value in cases where a person's thinking is not straight and perceptions are distorted. Hearing several people point out such mistaken concepts can be extremely powerful in producing change and setting misconceptions right. But in today's society, you can no longer rely on the opinions of the majority. If you are in group therapy, please do not abandon its benefits. But do find and use a sounding board to help you sift truth from error—for yourself within your own value system. And do not be afraid to stand up for and hold tightly to your beliefs when they are healthy and honest. Even though you may be depressed emotionally, that is no sign your values or thoughts are erroneous.

Moral or Spiritual Risks

At least twenty years ago a psychiatrist friend shared a grave concern with me. Today that concern is even greater, in my opinion, and I have seen the damage that has been done by the philosophy underlying this problem.

Every professional in the mental health field is keenly aware of the damage guilt causes people. Unfortunately, few therapists distinguish well between false guilt (in which people cannot clearly state what they have done wrong) and the healthy sense of remorse people experience when they have really done wrong.

What has happened, according to my friend, is a tragic therapeutic mistake. To alleviate the burden of guilt their patients bear, some therapists have helped them deny that their wrongdoings are actually very bad. They have, almost unconsciously, lowered the basic standards of right and wrong and helped callous the consciences of a great many people.

Let me hasten to emphasize that is *not* true of a great many therapists. But you need to be aware of this as a risk because most of us attempt to justify ourselves too readily anyway. This is one reason why I suggest that persons going into extensive counseling keep in touch with their clergy persons on a regular basis. I believe that contact can help protect against this risk.

Another moral risk must be addressed. A friend of mine is an excellent psychotherapist in the Midwest. She has found the courage to publish an experience she endured while in extended therapy in a distant state. The unscrupulous man who counseled her slowly intruded into her personal life until she gave in to his advances, and they became regularly sexually intimate. She now understands that she, seriously depressed and lonely, was vulnerable to his suggestions. But he was supposed to help in the restoration of her emotional health. He was entirely at fault for not only allowing, but also suggesting and encouraging these sexual liberties. Sadly enough, such situations do occur.

Be alert to any sexual innuendos of a personal sort from your counselor. In a world that seems to have gone sexually mad, both male and female, secular and religious, counselors may become inappropriate in their interactions with patients. Therapists are people, too, so I urge you to avoid paranoia or harsh judgments against anyone. Just keep your counseling on a professional basis, and if you feel uneasy with your therapist, speak up. Discuss your feelings, give examples of anything that contributes to your uneasiness, and ask for it to stop. You'll be doing yourself and your therapist a favor.

Sexual hang-ups and hurtful old experiences are commonly a part of any depressive state. Be careful not to wrongly lay on your therapist the blame for feelings that really come from half-forgotten memories from your past.

Whomever you choose and whatever the therapeutic avenues you pursue together, I offer you genuine hope. With expert help, personal honesty, great patience, and persistence, you can win the battle against depression. I wish for you the courage to work and the steadfastness to endure until you know the joy that the Creator wants you to know!

WORKS CITED

American Psychiatric Association. *The Diagnostic and Statistical Manual of Mental Disorders,* 3rd ed. American Psychiatric Association, 1980.

Blair, Eric [George Orwell]. *1984.* New York: Harcourt, 1949.

Braun, M., and Rekers, George A. *Sexual Eclipse.* Wheaton, Ill.: Tyndale House, 1981.

Burbach, D. J., and Borduin, C. M. "Parent-Child Relations and the Etiology of Depression." *Clinical Psychology Review,* vol. 40. 1986.

"Child-Care Dilemma, The." *Time.* 22 June 1987.

Comer, James P., M.D. "Young Suicides." *Parents.* August 1982.

Coopersmith, Stanley. *The Antecedents of Self-Esteem.* 1967. Reprint. Palo Alto, Calif.: Consulting Psychologists Press, Inc., 1981.

Couchman, Robert, M.Ed., Executive Director of Metro Toronto Family Service Association. "Against All Odds: An Examination of the Significant Other Person Factor in the Education of Disadvantaged Children." December 1975.

Erikson, Eric H. *Childhood and Society,* 2nd ed. New York: Norton, 1964.

Frankl, Dr. Victor. *Man's Search for Meaning.* New York: Simon and Schuster, 1984.

Fussell, James A. "Suicide among adolescents." *The Kansas City* [Missouri] *Star.* 29 June 1987.

Glasser, William. *Control Theory.* New York: Harper & Row, 1985.

Kashani, J. H., et al. "Depression in Children." *Archives of General Psychology,* vol. 40. November 1983.

Kosky, Robert, et al. *The Journal of Nervous and Mental Disease,* vol. 174, no. 9. 18 March 1986.

Marshall, Catherine. *Something More.* New York: McGraw-Hill, 1974.

Naisbitt, John. *Megatrends.* New York: Warner Books, Inc., 1982.

Rekers, George A. *Shaping Your Child's Sexual Identity.* Grand Rapids, Mich.: Baker Book House, 1982.

Stinnett, Nick, and DeFrain, John. *Secrets of Strong Families.* Boston: Little Brown and Company, 1985, a Berkley Book, 1986.

Trad, Paul V. *Infant and Childhood Depression.* New York: John Wiley & Sons, 1987.

Turnbull, Colin M. *The Mountain People.* New York: Simon and Schuster, 1972.

U.S. Center for Health Statistics. *Vital Statistics of the United States,* annual. U.S. National Center for Health Statistics, 1986, no. 122.

"User's Guide to Hormones, A." *Newsweek.* 12 January 1987.